Dedicated to Graham Smith (1956-2013)

Acknowledgements

In helping me compile this book, I would like to thank

Bill Taylor
Alison Thompson
Paul Hacker
Yoshinobu Ohta
Annette Turpin
Roy Gould
Neville Smith
Shaz Shahid

Special thanks to
Anthony Kirby for his help in the printing of this book.

和
心
会

Fighting Spirit

by Chris Thompson

with Bill Taylor

First published in 2015 by Kirby Publishing, in
association with BTKA Publishing, a division of The
British Traditional Karate Association.

To contact BTKA Publishing please email
cthompson1@btconnect.com

© Chris Thompson and Bill Taylor
Design by Paul Hacker

First Edition

British Library Cataloguing-in
Publication Data.
A catalogue record for this book is
available from the British Library.

Paperback Edition ISBN 978-0-9539338-6-0

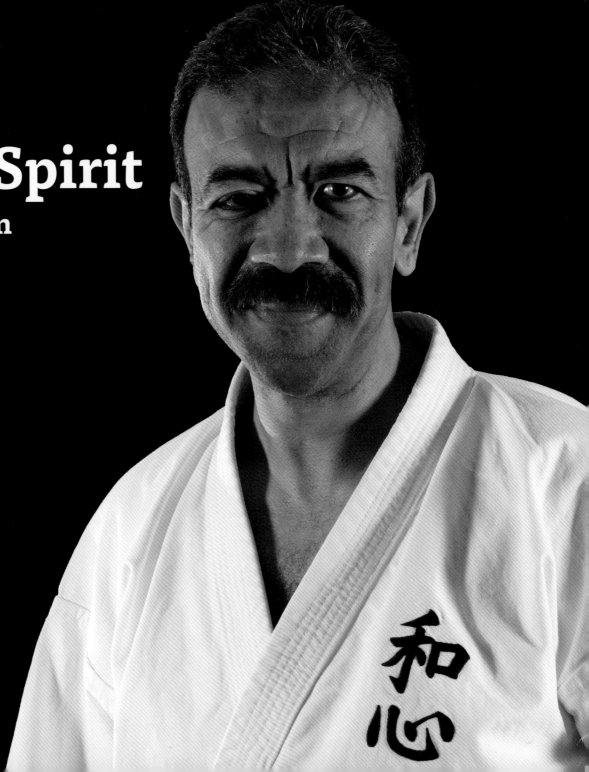

THE AUTHORS

Chris Thompson (8th Dan) started studying martial arts in the late 1960s when the Japanese first brought the style of Wado-Ryu karate to England. Sensei Thompson has been practising karate for forty-five years. He is chairman and chief instructor of the British Traditional Karate Association and teaches all over the world.

Bill Taylor is a journalist, writer and broadcaster. He has worked with the BBC, ITN and Channel Four as well as The Daily Telegraph, The Scotsman and The Sydney Morning Herald. Bill studies karate and also practises tai-chi and qi-gong.

CONTENTS

1. Against All the Odds: how a skinny, half-blind black teenager discovered his way in life with karate

2. The Judokan Years: The magic of karate - beginner to black belt and early influences.

3. Would You Sell Your Soul for a Black Belt? Why corruption and love of money never work in the long run.

4. The Bruce Lee & Steve McQueen Era: the first big split in English karate and a treasured meeting with Hironori Ohtsuka.

5. Different Masters, Other Styles: Hayashi, Nakayama, Yamaguchi, Mas Oyama, Kimura, Maeda, Yamamoto, Plee, Danny Connor, Michael Tse, Ticky Donovan.

6. Washinkai – Start of a New Era: testing the new karate syllabus behind closed doors, acceptance by Japan.

7. Way of the Empty Hand: the meaning of karate

8. Karate history: the Early Years

9.   Different Karate Styles and What They Offer
10. War Crimes & the Values of Karate.
11. The Washinkai Family
12. A Sense of Belonging
13. Children in Karate
14. "Hope In What You Can Achieve"
15. Life Skills for Soldiers, NHS Staff and Sixth Formers.
16. What Future for Karate in England?
17. Sport or Martial Art?
18. Why We Should Still Practise Martial Arts: the top ten benefits
19. What to Look For in a Good Karate Club
20. Is Karate Worth the Pain?
21. Still Crazy After All These Years

chapter 1
AGAINST ALL ODDS

和心会

On a hot and sticky summer evening in 1969, just as the Apollo space crew were making their final preparations to land on the Moon, I walked into a martial arts dojo for the first time. Strictly speaking, the house rules of the Judokan in west London said I was too young at fifteen to join their beginners' karate class. Children were not allowed in karate dojo at the time and women were actively discouraged. But they signed me up anyway and so began the adventure of my lifetime. The instructor with the black belt round his waist that night, Bob Wignall, had served his time working as a fairground bare knuckle boxer before taking up karate. As you might imagine, he was tough and strong and powerful, but he also turned out to be humble and courteous. Despite his hard fairground past, I never heard him swear. He was in every sense a gentleman. No one spoke at all in the dojo: total discipline, total silence. I was the youngest in the class, a tall skinny black kid from West London. Watching from the shadows were some of the first generation of Japanese judo and karate masters who had moved to Britain to teach their fighting arts in the West. By the time I sat the test for my first karate grading a few months later, almost all the adult students in that beginners' class had disappeared. The training was too tough. But I suspected I had found my destiny – my way. There was just an aura of magic about it. I was star struck. After more than forty-five years of teaching karate all over the world, the magic is still with me and I realise that I have had a lucky life.

It didn't look that way a few years earlier when a freak accident left me blind in one eye. Just three months into my first year at secondary school, I was messing around with a friend in the garden at home in Maida Vale, London. We put some potassium permanganate, Andrews Liver Salts and a little bit of everything into a screw-cap bottle and shook it up. There was an almighty explosion and I was left with a massive chunk of glass in my right eye. I was holding the bottle in my right hand and I'm lucky not to have lost my hand as well. I don't remember feeling any pain at all, but when my mother came running out she found me with my T-shirt completely covered in blood.

Throughout November 1965, I spent a month in the Western Ophthalmic Hospital in London's Marylebone Road and the surgeons fought hard to save my right eye. At one stage they were quite happy and hopeful that my sight would return. But not long after I left hospital and went back to Christopher Wren High School, one of the school thugs was doing the rounds of the playground flicking rubber bands at the faces of other students. He hit me in the injured eye and in an instant completely tore apart all the painstaking work the surgeons had done to give me back full sight. For the rest of my life, I was blind in my right eye.

Looking back, that accident helped set the path for my life in the martial arts. It certainly laid the foundation for some of the qualities I would need later as a teacher of

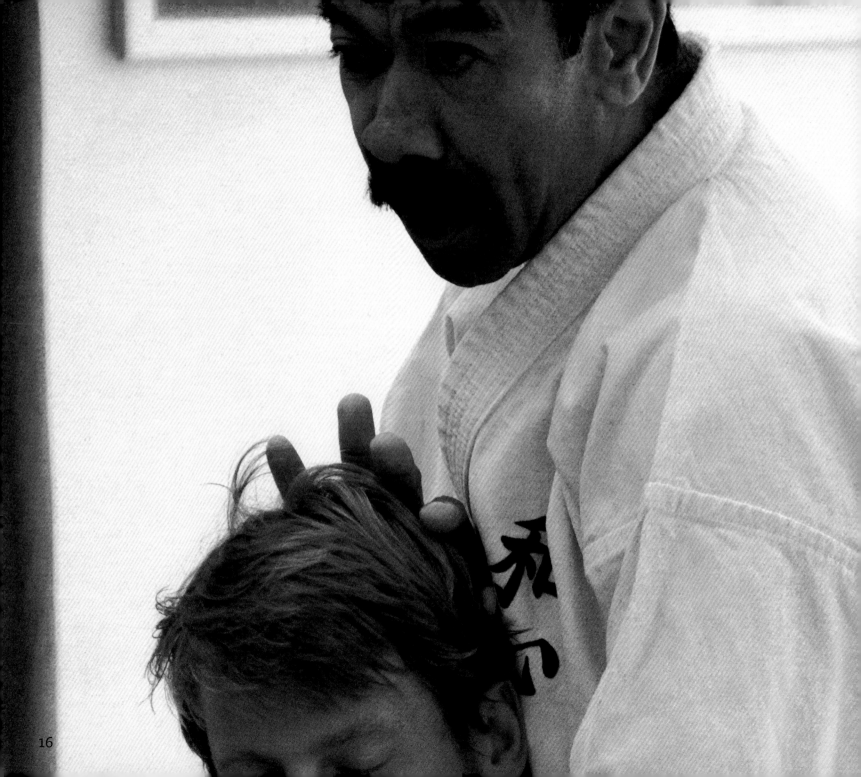

"You've got another eye," my dad said. "Use that."

karate: resilience, the capacity to turn fear and weakness into something strong and positive and the desire to get up and keep going after taking a big knock. This was certainly the attitude of my father, who was outwardly pragmatic about the whole affair, no doubt trying to instil in me the toughness and the will I would need to make something of myself in the world. "You've got another eye," he said. "Use that." There was no room at all to feel sorry for myself. I just had to get on with life. Much later, I came to understand you can use karate to overcome any disability if you have the desire to do it, if you want it badly enough.

Without realising it, the high-school teachers also helped me on my path. For nearly a year, they refused to let me take part in sport or anything physical, so anxious were they that I might be injured again. By the time I was fit and ready for the sports field, I wanted more than the usual cricket and rugby. For a while, I took up archery and became the London schoolboys' archery champion. But even though I enjoyed archery, I never felt quite

comfortable with it. I just knew it wasn't what I wanted.

This year of enforced recuperation – 1962 – was the era of the first James Bond films and my Jamaican-born parents knew well the area of the island where Dr No was filmed. The movie was the talk of our house long before it was released into British cinemas. We had another casual family interest in James Bond. Before my mother set up her own business, she worked as a seamstress for the Soho tailor Washington Tremlett and made some of Sean Connery's shirts. So it was with a special sense of anticipation that I went to see James Bond for the first time and, of course, like hundreds of thousands of other teenagers around the world, I became completely enchanted by Bond's ability to look after himself, even though I later realised that movie fighting was much

more about drama and entertainment than real combat. Little by little, for this adolescent boy finding his way back into life after serious injury, the longing to take up some form of karate lodged itself deep inside my heart and refused to go away, even though my parents still worried that martial arts might be too dangerous.

As a teenager, I was formed by the spirit of two very different decades, the Fifties and Sixties. My parents moved to London in the early 1950s, when Britain needed immigrants from the Commonwealth to do menial jobs in the growing post-war economy. They married not long after they arrived in the UK in a church at Seymours Place in London's West End. It was a time when Londoners often felt ambiguous – to say the least – about their new black neighbours. At St Luke's Primary School in Fernhead

Road, Maida Vale (where the comedian Norman Wisdom went to school), I was one of only three black faces in the playground.

I knew I was different and like so many other kids had to learn to deal with my share of bullying and name calling.

As soon as mum and dad arrived in England, they bought a terraced house at 37 Fordingley Road, Maida Vale, for £600. A sitting tenant already occupied half the house, so we lived in the other half. Money was very tight and the family relied on the rent from the sitting tenant as an essential part of the family income. While mum worked long hours to establish herself as a seamstress (she was the one with talent for business), my father – trained as a carpenter in Jamaica – worked as a porter with British Rail, spending much of his life stocking buffet and restaurant cars with crates of liquor. He held down that job until he retired. Everyday life was frugal, but I remember my childhood as a happy time with all the fun and hope of Sixties London opening up around me. Screaming Lord Sutch, that crazy, funny political maverick, was a patient at the Western Ophthalmic Hospital while I was a patient there in November 1965 and it amused me greatly to see all the nurses in such a flap. Mick Jagger and Keith Richard

"I was one of only
three black faces in
the playground."

set the background music to a rebellious decade and because my mother then worked in Savile Row, I was able to meet a long and impressive line of famous faces from the world of film and music. Inevitably, an occasional crate of British Rail booze found its way into our house and parties with Jamaican family friends became another, different part of the soundtrack of my adolescence.

When Cassius Clay won a gold boxing medal at the 1960 Rome Olympics, the world seemed to be changing as fast as I was growing up. My dad was a boxing fan and rightly forecast great success for the future Mohammed Ali. For myself, I learned that a black man could not only beat the world, but do it in style. I was mesmerised by his philosophy of not being put down: not just facing an opponent in the ring, but also standing up in life

Trophy success in the early years Chris Thompson's career. On the left, a young Sensei Thompson trains with Takao Yamamoto from Japan, an important influence on his career.

to the American government by opposing the draft to Vietnam. Much later in 1974, I was very proud to meet and shake hands with Mohammed Ali at London's Q Club in Praed Street, Paddington. I loved the speed at which he moved in on an opponent and then quickly away rather than waiting round for a slugging match – "move like a butterfly, sting like a bee" – and speed became an important weapon for me in early karate competitions.

Of course, being blind in one eye was a disadvantage on the karate competition mat, but I learned very early on that my weakness could be used against an opponent. I was blind-sided for quite some distance on the right side of my body and got into the habit of constantly turning and checking that weaker side, acutely conscious of the vulnerability. To protect the eye, I developed a very high

24

right-hand guard, which looked flamboyant then and even seemed like a come-on gesture, though it is much more common now. I had to understand my limitations. The last thing I wanted was another severe blow to the face that could have blinded me completely, so as I worked my way through national and international competitions my mantra became: "Keep your guard high and move fast. If someone lashes out – you don't want to be there." That is why I was so attracted by the Budo philosophy of using an attacker's energy against themselves. Yes, I was blind in one eye, but everything else worked. The disability made me sure to use every piece of armour I had available because I was so aware that one crucial part of my own sensory toolkit was missing. The greatest weapon I had was not strength but speed. If you're static, you're immediately at a disadvantage. If you can't move well, you can't be effective.

In a bizarre way, the eye injury could also be a real advantage in competition fighting. The distinctive scar and disfigurement put people off and actually intimidated a lot of opponents. Quite often in karate bouts, opponents fixed their gaze on the blind eye. They were mesmerised by it. As they stared, I moved in quickly and took advantage of their hesitation. I was very fast and the Japanese instructors encouraged me to use my speed.

An early Washinkai class at Canons Leisure Centre in Mitcham, Surrey. Far right is Steve Hawkins, the first student at the club

After more than forty-five years teaching karate, I still believe that you can turn any weakness into a strength if you want it badly enough. The biggest battle you will ever fight is in your own mind.

I first used karate to defend myself when I was fifteen. The bully boys were on the prowl again at Christopher Wren High School. A boy who had been badgering me regularly over four years grabbed me from behind in the playground. I turned round and immediately unleashed two uraken to each side of his face, uraken being a back-fist strike at full arm's length, a technique given power and momentum from the twisting motion of the hips. He fell like a sack of potatoes. I was still a white belt, the lowest rank of karate beginner, just a few months into my

training, but I learned two very important lessons that day. The success of the defence came not from strength, but from good technique delivered at speed without effort. And immediately, the rumour went round the school: "Keep away from Thompson. He can look after himself." My popularity went up. And I enjoyed a great boost to the ego born of stopping someone who'd been goading me for the first four years of high school. I was a potential victim no longer. I could stand tall and confident in my own black skin. The attacker wasn't seriously hurt, apart from severe damage to his reputation.

Thugs who look for trouble often have a sixth sense about who makes a willing victim, an easy target. If you shuffle around making yourself look as small as possible, with

"The greatest gift we can give our children is the capacity and the right to live without fear"

shoulders stooped and head down, you can attract the wrong kind of attention to yourself. It's the victim stance. Projecting an aura of inner confidence is often the best defence you have and the only protection you need: head held high looking straight out into the world, shoulders back and belly tucked in. That way, you are a less easy target. I do believe that if you are adept at martial arts you create an aura around yourself, a special layer of some kind, a confidence, a projection of energy through your body – chi or ki if you like to call it that. Victims don't have this aura or self-projection.

At the same time, in karate there is no first strike in thought or mind or deed. Respect, humility and courtesy are its hallmarks, as I learned in my first class at the Judokan that hot July night in 1969. It is the paradox at the heart of all martial arts. I believe that karate practised properly and taught well can help create safer communities and individuals. The greatest gift we can give our children is the capacity and the right to live without fear. We all strive for an environment where we feel safe. The bully mustn't win.

chapter 2
THE JUDOKAN YEARS

和
心
会

Karate the great leveller. On Chris Thompson's right at the Judokan in 1974 is the grandson of millionaire shipping tycoon Aristotle Onassis.

As I was growing up in the late Fifties and early Sixties in West London – on the borderlands of Maida Vale, Kilburn and Ladbroke Grove – I sensed a change in the atmosphere. A rough crowd, black and white, was moving into the area. We'd been burgled a few times and dad was being very careful. He kept a shillelagh in the house. Working as he did at British Rail in Paddington, lots of his friends were Irish. But it was more than that. As a black boy growing up in a London that was still overwhelmingly white, I was more than ever conscious of my race and colour. My father was native Jamaican and my mother was born into a Chinese family in Jamaica. Dad was verbally abused at work all the time. He wasn't a big chap,

but if he felt maligned he would hold his ground. When I was a child, it was comforting to know he could protect me. Violence seemed to be everywhere: the student riots in Paris, civil rights protests in the USA and the Troubles in Northern Ireland, with troops on the streets close to our own doorstep, not to mention the Notting Hill race riots in 1958 not far from the family home. As a young adolescent, my response to all this was: "I really want to be able to protect myself, to look after myself."

At the Judokan, there was no thought at all of race. A couple of black men had attended the beginners' karate class just before mine. No one batted an eyelid. In all sorts of different ways, the Judokan became my oasis. At the end of the four-week beginners' course, I was just elated. I knew this was something I loved, and I hope it loved me. It was my 'eureka moment'. Whether it was good luck or good timing, or a combination of both, I took up martial arts at the best possible moment, when leading Japanese karate instructors were lured to Britain to teach and also when the first generation of young English karate-ka were finding their way in a new and fascinating world.

Early years at the Judokan before the dojo received a facelift. The walls show years of blood, sweat and tears.

The man who literally opened the door to my new world and gave me so many early opportunities was the famous British judo champion Percy Sekine, who owned the

"Percy Sekine was a giant figure in the martial arts in Britain"

Percy Sekine outside the Judokan with his wife Hana Koizumi.

Judokan. He proposed and seconded me as a member of the club even though at fifteen I was well below the minimum age. Within a few minutes of walking through the door, I had borrowed an old and not too fresh judo suit, or gi, hanging in the dojo balcony and started my karate training.

Percy Sekine was a giant figure in the martial arts in Britain. Born in London in 1920 of an English mother and Japanese father, he started practising judo as a teenager at the Budokwai, the country's first martial arts club founded in 1918 by Gunji Koizumi. A judo black belt at the age of nineteen, Percy Sekine joined the RAF as a wireless operator and air gunner at the outbreak of World War II and was shot down over Holland. As a prisoner of war in Germany, he became something of a legendary figure when he organised judo classes for fellow inmates of Stalag 383 in Bavaria, negotiating with the camp guards for canvas and sacking to make judo suits and a makeshift tatami or judo mat. He escaped from prison camp three times, once "disguised" as a Japanese man.

After the war, Sekine married Hana Koizumi, daughter of the Budokwai founder, and in 1954 the couple set up the Judokan by converting two squash courts in a block of flats at Latymer Court, Hammersmith. It seemed to me a real dojo, very Japanese, with traditional tatami mats

and white walls, the two training areas separated by an open bar (Percy Sekine was very fond of a large late-night whisky after teaching his judo classes). Sekine represented Britain four times in international judo competitions during the 1940s and 1950s and was never beaten, despite the fact that at just over nine stone in weight he was usually fighting opponents much larger than himself. At seventh dan, he was at that time the highest ranking judo master outside Japan. Hanging on the white walls of the Judokan was a series of cartoons by the Evening Standard cartoonist Jak, one of the many personalities of the day who trained there, along with racing driver Stirling Moss, comedian Tommy Cooper, artist and sculptor Eduardo Paolozzi and David, Marquis of Queensberry. The Judokan may not have lived by Queensberry Rules, but it

The first instructors' meeting of Washinkai Karate. Top left is Graham Smith, to whom this book is dedicated.

was very much dominated by Percy Sekine's traditional and unfailing courtesy. For me, the place became a bit of a haven. It is where I first learnt the ethos of Budo, the traditional Japanese warrior code: to better yourself by helping others, to be respectful and courteous in all things. The Judokan also attracted former prisoners of war, many of whom had been helped and supported by Sekine during their enforced stay in Nazi camps. A regular visitor was Airey Neave MP, one of Margaret Thatcher's closest friends and advisers, who had survived the war by escaping from Colditz only to be killed by an Irish Republican car bomb at the House of Commons in 1979.

If Sekine opened the door to my first martial arts class (he died in 2010 at the age of ninety), it was karate instructor Bob Wignall who put me to work – in a very traditional style. We all got down to it right away, press-ups on our knuckles as the first drill to get the body warm, though it wasn't as bad as it sounds. The traditional Japanese tatami at the Judokan were very comfortable. "You can't do martial arts if you don't look after yourself," said Wignall. Fitness was just as important as technique: sit-ups, push-ups and belly crunches. The only equipment was your training partner. We routinely practised exercises that would be banned now. And there was great emphasis on basics. It wasn't uncommon to spend an entire hour-

long class practising one basic technique over and over again moving up and down the dojo in straight lines. Today's students complain about basics, but this constant repetition was highly beneficial and formed an important part of the philosophy of Wado-Ryu (the karate style I studied as a beginner): work hard and lay down strong foundations so you can react with speed and strength if needed under attack, when there is by definition no thinking time or preparation time. It wasn't until black belt that I realised how important these basic techniques, or kihon, are. It's all in those elementary steps. You can't progress until you have mastered the basics.

For all his very real courtesy, Bob Wignall was also a hard man: strong and inspiring, though he didn't strike me immediately as being very athletic. He spoke Japanese and everyone in class did exactly as he said, first time. No one spoke in the dojo. Silence was part of the discipline. Wignall had a great sense of power, strong but humble, and that is how I wanted to be. This tough Yorkshire man regularly teased us for being southern "Jessies" – softies – the first time I had heard the expression. Not surprisingly for someone who had worked as a fairground bare-knuckle boxer, he was very quick with his hands: elbows in and fists up. When you tried to block his arms during training drills, it was like stopping a lead pipe. He was a

Early days of Washinkai: Adrian Charles and Mick Stall battle it out in the late 1970s.

"forward man": in sparring or competition, he never went back and never retreated and that made him very popular indeed with the Japanese. Perhaps the most important lesson Bob Wignall taught us was tenacity. You kept going no matter what happened. It's something that still sticks with me today.

Within a few minutes of that first class, my borrowed and improvised karate gi was completely saturated in sweat, and it hadn't been especially clean to start with. But as I walked out into the bright, hot summer night I remember thinking: "I do love this. I'm not going to stop." Immediately, I dismissed all the action scenes I'd seen in the Bond movies for the entertainment they were. My dad had a hut at the end of the garden for carpentry and wood turning and whenever he began cutting into a new piece of work, he used to repeat almost as a mantra the traditional Chinese saying, "A journey of a thousand miles begins with a single step." That night, in 1969, I started my journey of a thousand steps and I'm still nowhere near the end of my road.

For me, karate had a magic element to it, definitely a mystique. You just never knew what the next part of the learning would be. These first steps in martial arts took place the year before my O-Level school exams, but

"For me, karate had a magic element to it, definitely a mystique."

despite all that I made a pledge to myself never to miss the twice weekly class. Karate dominated my life and in that sense, I was the one who stood out as an oddball. My mother encouraged me, but I'm not sure she was much impressed by martial arts. Not only that, family friends believed it was wrong to have any contact at all with the Japanese, so strong were the memories of Japanese cruelty to prisoners of war during World War II. All my father's friends hated the idea that I was practising a Japanese "sport". Even though I took up karate more than twenty years after the war ended, any talk of the courtesy at the heart of the ancient warrior code of Budo still left a very sour taste in the mouth for my parents' generation. I fully understand the hatred of the Japanese after World War II. When I began training in karate, the Japanese were still detested as a cruel race. But that is not my experience, and I know what it is like to be on the wrong end of a Japanese fist and foot. Percy Sekine, the man who gave me that first opportunity to study karate genuinely seemed to represent a bridge between two warring cultures: he

One of the Washinkai Karate classes run by Chris Thompson for the Inner London Education Authority (ILEA) in the late 1970s.

had an English mother and Japanese father, he fought for Britain in World War II against Germany and Japan, helped countless British prisoners of war, and then competed successfully for Britain on the international judo circuit. At the Judokan, he attracted British friends from the world of politics, sport, business and entertainment. He and his wife Hana – from a Japanese family herself – helped me enormously in my emerging life as a karate teacher. Sekine always lived absolutely by the traditional Budo values of respect for others and doing whatever he could to help others. This is the heart of the dilemma: I believe karate is indeed a martial art, but the mental and physical discipline demanded by its practice can somehow make you a stronger, more calm and respectful human being. For my first karate grading exam, in early 1970, I was sent to Judd Street in Kings Cross to the new headquarters

of Tatsuo Suzuki, the Japanese sensei who brought the Wado-Ryu style of karate to Britain in 1965. I was still only fifteen years old, the tallest in my family and the youngest in my karate class. I was shaking like a leaf in front of the huge crowd. The exam consisted of a few very basic techniques, but the Japanese instructor was looking for all the same qualities that make karate such a good companion in everyday life: strong stances, movement, balance, mobility and stability rolled into one, powerful kicks and punches. You won't give in. You won't just fold when someone shouts at you. You hold your ground. Will your techniques be effective? Whatever the level of grading exam, it's always the same questions. It's a lot about confidence.

I received a first class pass in that 8th kyu exam, still the

lowest of lowly beginners with a single black stripe on my white belt, but I was absolutely ecstatic. I think that was it: the seed was sown and I pretty much knew that practising and teaching karate would be my destiny. Karate was already dominating my life. One of the major reasons for not going to university was so I could keep going to the dojo. Bob Wignall pushed me on, with a new grading every three months. As I moved up through the ranks, I started training with many of the first-generation Japanese karate instructors. Within a year, Percy Sekine asked me to start teaching karate and I was already doing well in competition. At the age of eighteen, after three years of non-stop training, I presented myself at the London headquarters of the UK Karate Federation for grading as a first-degree black belt, shodan. The examiner was Tatsuo Suzuki himself. To be honest, I don't remember anything about the grading at all, I seemed to just race through it. When I passed, I felt I could have walked on the moon. There was definitely a buzz in the air when I went back to the Judokan. The moment I had dreamt of was suddenly here. Everything was happening. I was in the middle of A-levels and about to start my working life with the British Bank of the Middle East in the City. But I couldn't afford to be too sure of myself just yet – I had to ask my mother for the £15 grading fee to pay Sensei Suzuki!

Wado Ryu Winter Course for students of Sensei Tatsuo Suzuki at the Elephant and Castle in London in 1973 - John Moreton in the background, Chris Thompson far right corner with his back to the camera.

chapter 3
WOULD YOU SELL YOUR SOUL FOR A BLACK BELT?

師範クリス・トンプソン

和心会

Chris Thompson presented with his 7th Dan at Highbury College, Portsmouth 1998.

Now I wore the black belt I had dreamed of, but what did it mean? The black belt is simply a new beginning, a signpost on the long, slow and hard road to self-improvement and understanding. There are no real short cuts, whatever your social status or wealth. Indeed, that is one of the attractions of karate. In the training hall, everyone is equal. The dojo should be one of the few places in modern life where money or social status do not and cannot have the last word. From the first day in my life in karate, I experienced no discrimination on the basis of my colour or social background. Being young in the Sixties certainly helped with all that.

"My friend said he had been offered £10,000 for a registered and certified black belt."

Even though the martial arts were free of race or class barriers, they certainly did have their share of financial corruption. Throughout my life in karate there have been many stories of people bribing their way to a black belt. In the early 1970s, it was said that £750 was the expected rate for buying a black belt, and that was a great deal of money at the time. My friend Danny Connor, one of the first people to set up a Wado-Ryu club in Britain and an important figure in my own life in martial arts, said he had been offered £10,000 for a registered and certified black belt. At the same time, I knew of a 5th Dan Black Belt being "bought" for £5,000. In the early Seventies, it was not uncommon to hear about people getting black belts for money, including karate-ka I knew were well below standard.

Certainly, this much coveted rite of passage is a precious commodity. In some countries, a black belt in karate allows the holder to bypass military service and make a living as a professional instructor, so the bribe might well be seen as a worthwhile investment on the part of the individual involved. But money proves nothing. It flies in the face of all the values of karate. It certainly doesn't make you a better teacher or human being. Most people who followed the corrupt road have quietly but surely

disappeared. They are found out very quickly and it turns out to be an expensive mistake. But there's no doubt that money and politics have tarnished martial arts.

If you want to continue karate after being awarded that first degree black belt, then the training is never ending. The benefits are slow. Not much comes easy and nothing comes quickly. That may not be a very modern message. But a life lived in this way gives the karate-ka personal qualities that money can't ever buy: tenacity, mental conditioning, physical strength and agility, respect for yourself and others. It brings the best out in you.

To wear a black belt well, you also need a high level of maturity. Today, around three-quarters of karate students in the United Kingdom are children. When I began training, children were not allowed in the dojo at all. Now, they bring great energy and talent to the martial arts. Without these children as students, karate would have faded out of the mainstream of British life. But you still cannot and should not fake or rush the kind of maturity needed to wear a black belt, however strong the pressure may be from ambitious parents or students.

Fighting Spirit during the Instructors' class at the Judokan in 1978

I remember a winter course run by Sensei Tatsuo Suzuki

in London's Soho where a black belt student aged around twelve was hit by another boy and burst into tears. That makes a mockery of the whole black belt system. Children cannot possibly have the necessary level of maturity, understanding or awareness of the realities of street life. In my own British Traditional Karate Association, the minimum age for receiving a black belt is fourteen and it will not be ratified until the student is sixteen. This is also the standard set by the World Karate Federation. How can you have a black belt under the age of fourteen? To see a ten year old black belt walking around the dojo swearing – as I have done – defeats everything we stand for. Karate is never a quick fix, for children and adults alike. Good karate demands persistence and constant practice. But if the rewards are slow coming, then they also last a lifetime.

Gichin Funakoshi, one of the founding fathers of modern karate in Japan, was the first karate sensei to give his students a dan-grade rank. He, in turn, copied the system created by Jigoro Kano, the founder of modern-day judo. However, Funakoshi made it very clear that a student who received the first-dan rank of shodan was simply beginning a new phase in a lifetime of training. The black belt is just the first rung on the ladder of learning. That is the point I had reached at the age of eighteen, with a whole new life and world opening up before me. And the way forward was often anything but smooth.

chapter 4
THE BRUCE LEE & STEVE McQUEEN ERA

和心会

The Seventies was a fantastic decade, both in English karate and in my own life as a young martial arts teacher. Everyone seemed alive with a sense of new opportunity. It was a time of improvisation, creativity and exploration. Everything was in a very embryonic state. Even though all karate styles had a set syllabus steeped in the Japanese tradition, it was a period when we could and did create new and better ways of doing things. The bench marks were not yet set in stone. The Bruce Lee phenomenon brought long queues to the door of all martial arts dojos, including the Judokan. It meant that while the boom lasted I could give up my job at the British Bank of the Middle East and teach karate professionally. My home life

was changing, too. I married my high school sweetheart, Barbara Grant, and our first child was on the way. By the age of twenty, I had a new career, a new family, new home in Mitcham, Surrey, and a mortgage. However, for all the change and excitement, it was also to become a decade of turmoil, disruption and disillusionment in English karate. Some of the Japanese masters we had looked up to and learned from were about to fall from grace.

The Bruce Lee cult changed the public perception of the martial arts, almost overnight. I first heard of Lee in the early Seventies at film studios on the outskirts of

Chris Thompson's first wife Barbara with his son Christian - at home beside dad's first ever makiwara board.

London. The Judokan and the Budokwai were regularly asked to provide security at events such as Miss World and for Hollywood stars filming in England. It was on one of those working visits to the big film studios that I met Steve McQueen, who was in London visiting friends. I was still a teenager and talking to a superstar. McQueen, a thoughtful and philosophical man for all his big-screen reputation as an action hero, had trained with Bruce Lee and talked about the techniques he had learned from him. That was the first time I had heard the name. It wasn't until those first Kung Fu films appeared that I understood fully what Steve McQueen was talking about.

Bruce Lee was an exceptional martial artist, mentally as well as physically. I don't think he realised what he did for the world of karate. Before his films, people who practised the martial arts were seen as outsiders, a bunch of eccentrics, to put it politely. Bruce Lee made it mainstream. He glamorised it. And he always brought his strong personal philosophy into the movies alongside the action. Before Bruce Lee came on the scene, my karate class at the Judokan had an average of six to ten people. After the release of his film Enter the Dragon, the class was packed and the Judokan had new and eager students queuing outside the front door and along the street, partly because there were very few Kung-Fu clubs in England at the time. Enter the Dragon became a cinema sell-out across Britain, Europe and the USA. Lee died just a month before the movie first appeared on our screens in 1973. He was only thirty-two years old, but his cult status attracted new people to the martial arts all over the world. His legacy is well and fairly summed up by his biographer Bruce Thomas: "Bruce Lee lived an extraordinary life: he bridged cultures, revolutionised the martial arts, taught a fierce philosophy of individualism, remade the image of the Asian man in the West and, in the process, became unforgettable."

A lot of Bruce Lee's techniques just don't work for me, but he was still an extremely important influence. The martial art he created, Jeet Kune Do, was grounded in Chinese Wing Chun theory, but at the same time he borrowed liberally from other fighting arts in many parts of the world. His attitude was: "Whatever you practise, it won't be effective if it's not natural." He wanted to get away from the "only one way" philosophy of traditional martial arts masters. And in that, he was certainly right! If karate had been taught in a less authoritarian and brutal way, I think we would have had many more students than we did. Of course, Lee was also a major influence financially. Thanks to the aura of glamour he brought to the martial arts, I was now earning more money teaching karate part-time in the evenings than I did working a forty-hour week at the bank. Although the boom years didn't last long, the Bruce Lee phenomenon did help to establish me in my new life as a professional karate teacher. If it hadn't been

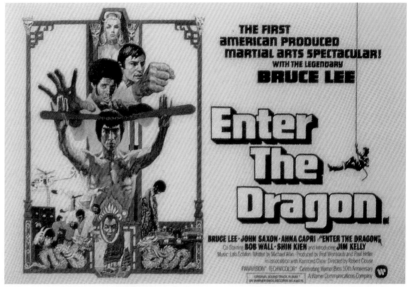

65

"At the heart of the upheaval were corruption, politics and money."

for him, I would still be teaching a small handful of people two evenings a week in the Judokan.

However, at the same time the Bruce Lee legend was attracting a whole new generation of followers to the martial arts across the world, traditional karate in England was descending into total turmoil. One of the most important men at the centre of the chaos was my own teacher and mentor Tatsuo Suzuki, the Japanese master who brought the Wado-Ryu style of karate to Britain in 1965. At the heart of the upheaval were those ancient, familiar foes: corruption, politics and money.

Suzuki's life and spirit were defined by the Second World War, for good and ill, like so many men and women of his generation. When he was a boy, his family fled to the countryside from their home in Yokohama to escape American bombing raids. By the time they returned to the city after the war, the Americans had become the occupying power in Japan. Suzuki had studied kendo at school, but as a teenager he became attracted to karate. "After the war," he said, "we were not allowed swords, so I looked for a martial art without weapons. In judo, it was always the big guy who won, but karate was different. With speed, timing and good spirit I could defeat any opponent large or small. Post-war Japan saw the Japanese people embrace everything American: baseball, Coke, Elvis. I wanted to give the world something Japanese. I

Far left in the back row is Mark Lester, who took up karate after making an international reputation as a child actor. Front left is Shaz Shahid, one of the most successful competition fighters ever taught by Chris Thompson.

67

decided to become a great martial artist so I could teach the world about the Japanese spirit."

He first studied karate as a teenager at the YMCA in Yokohama. "The Americans had banned all martial arts, so we had to call karate 'Japanese boxing'. I trained at the YMCA for about six months before we had to move on. We would train wherever we could, in gardens or fields, in the rain and snow, anywhere that Americans could not find us." Soon Suzuki was travelling several times a week to Tokyo to train with the founder of Wado-Ryu karate, Hironori Ohtsuka. "He was a truly great man. Away from karate he was a gentleman, but inside the dojo he was like a true samurai. He would train with us as well as teach us. Many of his senior black belts had returned from the war. They were tough both physically and mentally. The fighting in those lessons was extremely hard. In the old days, fighting was different than it is today. There were no rules. Any technique was allowed: kicks to the groin, strikes to the eyes or throat." Karate contests between opposing university teams erupted into tribal blood baths, cheered on by the crowd, with regular broken bones and missing teeth, until the leaders of Japan's different karate styles got together to create the first competition rules. But the young Tatsuo survived and thrived and was awarded his third-dan black belt by Ohtsuka at the age of nineteen. In the Sixties, now a fifth dan, he was sent

abroad to become one of the founding fathers of karate in the West. Over the next forty years and more he succeeded in establishing the Wado-Ryu style in Britain, throughout Europe and in many other parts of the world. His training, background and fierce dedication to karate made Tatsuo Suzuki a tough, brutal and uncompromising teacher of the martial arts. The bitter English winters didn't help. "I missed Japan. I was living in a bed-sit that would get so cold that it would be impossible to sleep. I would have to train to warm up before going to bed."

However much Tatsuo Suzuki became a legendary figure in the karate world, he had also made a lot of enemies by the mid-Seventies, not least among his own Japanese assistant instructors. They felt they were being manipulated, effectively used as teaching "slaves". Suzuki brought his instructors to England on student visas, but then sent them all over the country working for him, teaching karate on his behalf. He charged them rent, but also took for himself and his organisation much of the money they earned from teaching. The system was completely flawed. Suzuki wanted money for everything. I understand his longing for the status and money he could command in the West. He had grown up in Japan defeated and destroyed by war. But now his own Japanese assistants were turning against him.

A growing number of Japanese karate teachers wanted to be in London. The city was the epicentre of life. The new generation of Japanese instructors had developed a taste for Western life and were less prepared to follow the old master-servant relationship that was the historic tradition in the martial arts in Japan.

I finally knew things were falling apart when I arrived at the Judokan one afternoon to find that all Suzuki's Japanese assistants had raided the bar in the dojo and were drunk as skunks, in the midst of a wild protest against their master. By the time I reached home that evening, Hana Sekine – wife of the Judokan's founder – was on the phone asking me what was happening. Wado-Ryu karate in England was splitting apart. I became very disillusioned by the corruption. I thought I was born for karate, and karate was made for me, but the Wado-Ryu style that had been my first taste of the martial arts was now split by faction fighting and resentment. Tatsuo Suzuki had broken away from the people who originally invited him to Britain and set up his own organisation, the UK Karate Federation, which had its early headquarters in Judd Street in Kings Cross. A few weeks after the drunken protest, I sent a group of my own students to Judd Street for grading and they all failed the exam, every one of them! I realised that Suzuki had launched a vendetta against the Judokan, scene of the drunken protest against him. Normally, the Japanese

pass rate at gradings could be as low as twenty per cent, which meant repeat exam fees and more income for the instructors, but seeing everyone fail was a first. It was all a bit of racket. At clubs in the north of England, non-Japanese black belts were not allowed to grade their own students, ensuring the significant grading fees remained with Suzuki. The northern Wado-Ryu clubs were feeling angry, with their loyalty stretched to the limit and their respect for Suzuki constantly undermined by his love of money. Greed and corruption were starting to infiltrate English karate, causing deep resentment at the grass roots.

At this turbulent time, a major influence on my own life in karate was Tadayuki Maeda, one of the Japanese instructors involved in the drunken protest against Suzuki. Maeda was scathing in his criticism of his master. A former all-Japan karate champion, Maeda was awe

Sensei Tatsuo Suzuki (centre), the man who brought Wado-Ryu karate to Britain in the late 1960s. On the right is Katsumi Kobayashi, one of the most important influences on the young Chris Thompson.

> *"...two generations were being torn apart and so were my loyalties."*

inspiring to watch and I used to train with him wherever he was in the UK, travelling all over England just to learn from him. He was a brilliant karate-ka with beautiful techniques. On the competition mat, he always seemed to know where his opponent would be next. He could read your mind and he was a perfect technician. He was a perfectionist and became my own yardstick for what a great karate-ka should be. There was no brutality involved at all in his karate. Suzuki was brutal to the core, and I understand why. His experience growing up in post-war Japan probably meant he had to be uncompromisingly tough to make his way to the top in his chosen life. But the reality was that two generations were being torn apart and so were my loyalties. This was not only a split in the karate world I knew, but a deep divide between pre-war and post-war generations, a conflict that had been played out in almost every walk of life during the Sixties, not least in college campuses and on the streets.

Another member of that original group of Japanese Wado-Ryu instructors, Meiji Suzuki (no relation to Tatsuo Suzuki), then left the fold to become chief instructor of a new organisation based in London, the Amateur Karate Association. With the Wado-Ryu organisation in Britain split into two major factions, I was torn between different worlds and rival organisations. I had trained hard to execute what I thought were the "flawless" techniques of the Japanese teachers. But two of my sensei who had become close personal friends were now in separate camps, teaching slightly different ways of doing things. My loyalties were increasingly divided. For a time, I tried to hedge my bets by training with both organisations, only to be constantly corrected by different instructors. I had to make a choice. Then, quite by chance, another moment of magic arrived in my life. The creator and founder of Wado-Ryu karate, Hironori Ohtsuka, walked into the Judokan when I was teaching a class there. Already in his early eighties by this time, he had a profound effect on my future life.

Ohtsuka, with his son Jiro, had been invited to London as a guest to open the 1975 national championships of the UK Karate Federation, Tatsuo Suzuki's new organisation. While he was in London, he asked Suzuki – his former student – to show him a Japanese-style dojo in London and both men came to the Judokan. While I was teaching,

Hironori Ohtsuka (right), creator and founder of Wado-Ryu Karate.

I saw them out of the corner of my eye. All of a sudden, there was a whispered commotion and he was there. After the class, Sensei Ohtsuka came on to the tatami and suddenly I had a great opportunity to go right back to the source of my karate and ask some fundamental questions. Percy Sekine helped. This tiny little man was a giant figure in the martial arts world. Given that he had created the style of karate I practised, all my questions were about how and why certain techniques emerged in the way they did. He spent nearly an hour explaining the origins and inspiration for the martial arts techniques still being taught to new students in London. Ohtsuka talked about that central pillar of Wado-Ryu karate: the need to deflect the opponent's attacking power – don't absorb it. Use the attacker's energy against himself. Don't fight force with force. His core philosophy was: "If you don't feel comfortable with a technique, don't do it." As a martial arts student, he said, you must do what feels natural to you. This seemed a world away from the authoritarian teaching of traditional instructors whose method could be summed up as: "Copy me, do as I say and don't ask any questions." The Japanese come from a do-what-you're-told culture. Of course, Ohtsuka made complete sense. He had broken away from the martial arts establishment in Japan to create his own special way of doing things. He himself had merged traditional ju-jitsu with the emerging art of karate in a way that did not

"This tiny little man was a giant figure in the martial arts world."

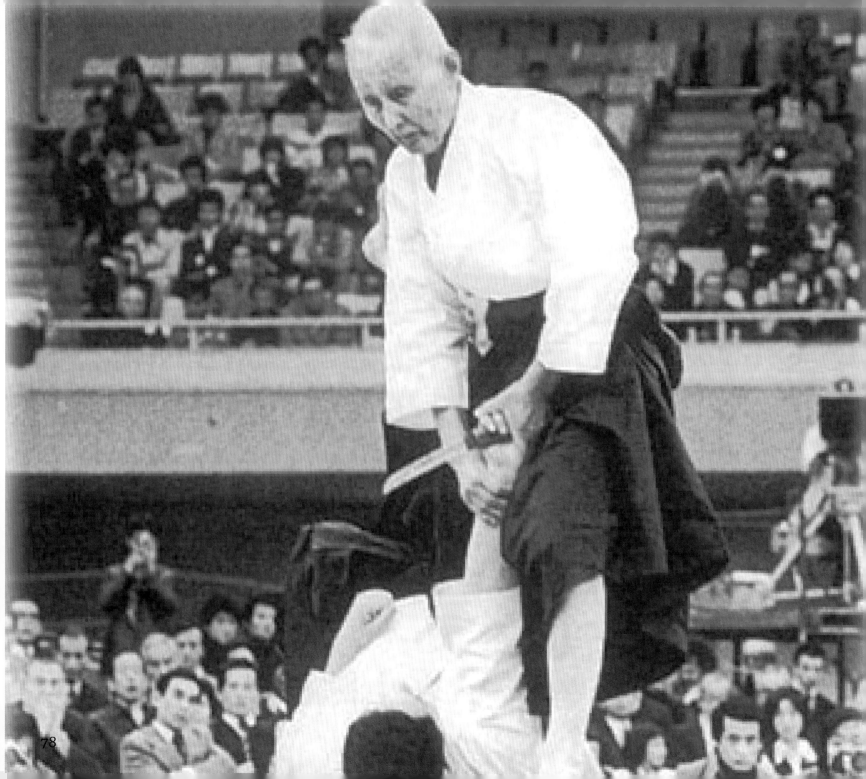

always please the purists in Japan. His words encouraged me to think for myself and follow the path that seemed right to me. I shouldn't be a stooge or practise karate parrot-fashion. From that meeting with Ohtsuka, I came to understand more completely the Budo philosophy of Shu-ha-ri, the continuously turning cycle of learning and progression in all martial arts:

- Shu – obey orders and copy instructions to build a strong technical foundation.
- Ha – explore, question and study the underlying basis for any teaching.
- Ri – transcend your teacher to find a way that is right and natural for you.

Like the best teachers, Sensei Ohtsuka came along just at the right time. Without knowing it, he encouraged me to step outside the politics, corruption, money and greed that were tearing English karate apart to explore a better way. Within one training session, Ohtsuka set my life in karate on a new and different path. Despite the generations between them, his philosophy also found an echo in the beliefs of Bruce Lee: "Whatever you practise, it won't be effective if it's not natural." Both Ohtsuka and Bruce Lee had a strong impact on the development of Washinkai, the new Wado-based style of karate I created over the coming few years.

nsei Ohtsuka demonstrates
fence against a knife attack.

chapter 5
EXPLORING OTHER STYLES AND DIFFERENT MASTERS

81

和心会

Loyalty can sometimes blind you to the truth. For several years, I had accepted without too much question my early instructors' teaching that Wado-Ryu karate was the best in the world. When Tatsuo Suzuki fell from grace even in the eyes of his own Japanese lieutenants, I felt free to explore a much wider world in the martial arts. In these early days, I tried out everything and took the opportunity to study with and learn from a wide range of Japanese and Western teachers who were indeed among the best in the world, irrespective of their different styles. Star struck I may have been with my new life in karate, but I was also determined to seek out the truth for myself, especially after such a period of financial and ideological double dealing. Paradoxically, the man who gave me the freedom to make this new journey in the martial arts was the founder of Wado-Ryu, Honori Ohtsuka: a genteel old man, peaceful, tiny in stature, not at all aggressive, very tai chi in his way, far from dictatorial, but nevertheless quietly insistent that I had an obligation to do what seemed right, natural and truthful to me on and off the training mat. Over the next few years I studied and trained with Japanese leaders of all the major foundation karate styles to spread to the west: Shotokan, Goju-Ryu, Shito-Ryu, Kyokushinkai as well as my own Wado-Ryu. Many of them were attracted to London by the city's growing reputation as an international centre for the martial arts. It was an opportunity not to be missed. Over the last twenty years and more all of these leading figures in karate have died and passed into memory. In a lucky life, I am fortunate to have been able to learn from them all.

When I first saw Teruo Hayashi, I was mesmerised by his aura of strength. Perhaps that is not surprising for a man of his background. A student of Kenwa Mabuni, one of the founders of Shito-Ryu karate, Hayashi had spent part of his youth touring martial arts dojos in Okinawa, the island half way between China and Japan which became the birthplace of modern karate. He followed the traditional Japanese custom of dojo yaburi, where he would walk in to a strange training hall and challenge anyone there to fight, including the sensei. If he was beaten, he would stay and learn all he could from that dojo before moving on. When I saw him in London as a much older man, he

Chris Thompson with Sensei Teruo Hayashi, leader of Shito-Ryu Karate and a major influence on the development of Washinkai Karate katas.

84

still radiated an enormous sense of power.

Also in the mid-Seventies, Masatoshi Nakayama came to London and packed out the Crystal Palace arena with followers eager to witness his immensely strong martial arts expertise. Nakayama was the internationally renowned Japanese master of Shotokan, the most widely practised style of karate in the world. He helped establish the Japan Karate Association in 1949, and wrote many textbooks which are still widely read today. He was one of the most important influences in creating a truly international interest in karate. When Nakayama gave demonstrations, it was almost as if the floor rocked. He had great power and superb technique. Taking part in the demonstration that day was Keinosuke Enoeda, known as The Tiger, a student of Nakayama who went on to become an equally formidable chief instructor of the Japan Karate Association in London. Today, Shotokan in Britain is led by the New Tiger, Sensei Yoshinobu Ohta, who for his own part brings a real aesthetic beauty to his techniques as well as power.

Another inspiration was Gogen 'The Cat' Yamaguchi, who had studied as a young man with Chojun Miyagi, the founder of Goju-Ryu karate. As a prisoner of war in a Soviet concentration camp during World War II, Yamaguchi escaped hard labour by teaching karate to his camp guards. There was even a legend that he had fought – and defeated – a live tiger during his time in the Soviet prison camp. He was just over five feet tall. I trained with his son Goshi at a dojo in Old Street, London, while the great man cast a watchful and critical eye over everything. Like Nakayama, The Cat played a pivotal role in popularising karate across the world. In April 1977, he told a French martial arts journalist: "Even today, young man, if you were to face me in combat, I would be able to determine in a second the strength of your Ki [life energy]. Immediately, I would know if you were a good opponent. It is this quality … which has given me the name of The Cat." I learned a great deal from Goju-Ryu. They were close fighters, crowding you during sparring and blocking at close range, then defending themselves fiercely in retreat. They fought cagily.

At Wembley and Crystal Palace, I also saw Mas Oyama, the founder of the Kyokushinkai style of full-contact karate. He, like Tatsuo Suzuki, was another legendary hard man shaped by war. Born in what is now South Korea, he began studying martial arts at the age of nine when his teacher was a seasonal worker on his sister's farm in Manchuria. He moved to Japan in 1938 and studied with kamikaze pilots at one of the aviation schools of the Imperial Japanese Army. In a later interview for TV in Japan, he said: "I lost many friends during the war. The very morning of their departure as kamikaze pilots, we had breakfast together and in the evening their seats were empty. After the war

ended, I was angry, so I fought as many US military as I could." Picking fights with American military police meant his picture was on the wall of every police station in Tokyo, so a supporter suggested he leave on a mountain retreat for his safety and sanity. He finally returned to open his own dojo in Tokyo in 1953 and eventually developed the hard-hitting practical style of karate that became known as Kyokushinkai, which has dojos all over the world. His book What is Karate? has sold more than a million copies all over the world.

Throughout the Seventies in London, I trained with senior students of Shigeru Kimura, one of the founding fathers of Shukokai karate. I was becoming increasingly

Gogen 'The Cat' Yamaguchi founder of Goju-Ryu Japan Karate.

attracted by the more relaxed, natural and aesthetic style of a new generation of Japanese martial artists including Kobayashi, Kitamura, Tadayuki Maeda and Takao Yamamoto.

It wasn't only the Japanese who were influential. The French judo exponent Henri Plee set up Europe's first karate dojo in 1955 after a visit to Japan. Not only did his students practise a fiercely high standard of karate, but they used their cool-down time in training to discuss the history of martial arts. In my imagination, here at last was welcome evidence of a further break from the traditional Japanese teaching style of: "Copy your teacher, do what you're told and don't ask questions." I didn't want to be a

Mas Oyama, founder of Kyokushinkai Karate

stooge. I knew that if I was to have any credibility as a teacher, then I had to know what I was teaching. I didn't want to be a parrot – and, to be honest, a lot of the Japanese martial artists were parrots. They didn't know the answers to basic questions about martial arts history and the development of technique. The myth of Wado as the only style worth learning was being well and truly shattered.

Another myth – of the Japanese as the undisputed master race of the art of karate – was also swept away in 1975 when England won its first world championships, held that year in Long Beach, California. Karate was becoming truly international. One member of that victorious England team was David ('Ticky') Donovan, who went on to coach the England squad for more than thirty years, leading them to six world titles. He had established early on his own style of Ishin-Ryu karate and I trained at one of his dojos in East Ham to try out the subtleties of yet another way.

The more I studied the history of karate, the more I realised that its roots and influences lay not only in Japan, but deep in Chinese history. Sensei Danny Connor from Manchester, who set up one of the first British Wado-Ryu clubs in the mid-Sixties, was moving over to Kung-Fu and Tai-Chi. He showed me the historical Chinese traditions behind Japanese karate techniques and forms. He introduced me to one of the teachers of Bruce Lee. I also met Michael Tse, a Hong Kong policeman who eventually moved to Britain to teach tai-chi. Michael gave me my first introduction to the ancient Chinese art of qi-gong.

Another British martial artist who chose the Chinese way was Paul Crompton. He had studied boxing, judo, karate, Kung-Fu and aikido before devoting his life to practising and teaching Tai-Chi. In the Sixties he had a martial arts shop in Fulham Road in London and published a popular magazine called 'Karate and Oriental Arts'. In 1988, he published my own first book, Essentials of Wado-Ryu Karate.

Every branch of martial arts – whichever nation and culture it comes from – has its differences and its fierce rivalries. That is human nature. Many karate-ka claim to have followed the true way with the best teachers in the perfect historical lineage. But during my searching "wilderness years", I discovered many different paths to the same paradoxical truth. An effective martial art has to be highly realistic in its training and techniques as well as truthful and honest in its practice. It has to train its followers to live not only with a strong and courageous heart, but also with a peaceful mind and spirit. I have always believed this to be an ideal worth following. This was the inspiration for Washinkai, the new Wado-based style of karate I was about to trial and create. I was still only in my mid-Twenties.

chapter 6
WASHINKAI: START OF A NEW ERA

和心会

At the Yotsuya Dojo in Tokyo 1988. On Sensei Thompson's left is Seiji Sugimoto, a world champion in Shotokan Karate.

My breakaway from the dominance and control of the original generation of Japanese teachers in the UK was the most important period in my life in karate. I was not aware I was about to form a new style. It just developed. And leaving the Japanese wasn't just an ego trip on my part. There were six or seven leading British teachers of martial arts who felt exactly the same way: they believed they were giving out too much money to the Japanese masters and learning nothing new. Several of them came to me and said: "This is not right. What are you going to do about it?" For myself, I can never criticise the time I spent learning Wado-Ryu with the Japanese instructors, nor the style itself. The knowledge they passed on to me was priceless and I made many friends. But it was time to search for a new home.

By the mid-Seventies, I had left Tatsuo Suzuki's organisation and I trained for a couple of years under the umbrella of the new Amateur Karate Association. Meiji Suzuki, the former Japan Universities Karate Champion who went on to co-found the martial art Mugendo, was then chief instructor of the AKA. Within the space of a few years, I had achieved Second Dan and then Third Dan black belt and studied with some of the world's leading exponents of all the major karate styles. I was introduced to tai chi and qi gong and touched on judo, aikido and tae kwon do. But nothing could beat the hold of karate. It just seemed to latch on to me. It still does!

I admired many aspects of all the karate schools I trained with, but felt that none could offer exactly what I was looking for. Slowly, the Washinkai style of karate began to emerge, a name suggested by the Japanese girlfriend of my close friend and collaborator Graham Smith.

- Wa – for harmony, to acknowledge my roots in Wado-Ryu.
- Shin – for heart, mind and spirit working together as one, but also for truth, extremely important to me after all the disillusionment brought on by the petty corruption and lies of recent years.
- Kai – for group, organisation or home.

Canons Karate Club in the early days of Washinkai in 1986.

In the beginning, Washinkai was a name to identify with rather than a new style. But over a period of several years, a complete martial arts system emerged capable of taking the student from beginner to first black belt and beyond. After its launch in 1977-78, Washinkai was quickly recognised and approved by karate's ruling authorities as a complete fighting system.

For a whole year, I worked on the different and wide-ranging techniques I had learned from all the karate styles and different martial arts I had studied. I tried to weed out failures in my own practice and transform them into beneficial techniques. A small group of friends and fellow martial artists worked with me to stress test the new Washinkai system: Graham Smith (who died in 2013), Colin Inwood – who had started as a beginner with me in 1975 – and two young Japanese martial arts stylists, Hironori Goda and Takao Yamamoto. Behind locked and closed doors, we tried and tested everything thousands of times. We made people attack us vigorously to find out how realistic our techniques were. Graham Smith tested our defences and blocks using a razor sharp knife. We used to hold sessions lasting hours going through everything.

Many of the Wado-Ryu moves were still stuck in the 19th Century, so we dismissed a lot of them as archaic. We were still being fed techniques that had a benefit historically,

Friend, guide and mentor: Takao Yamamoto in action in 1984

but not today. Useless moves continued just because they were in the syllabus. At the same time, we incorporated some tai chi and qi gong. We were searching for a karate style that was realistic and effective. We got it all down to things that worked. Over the years, I had trained with quite a few World War II veterans who would say of some traditional karate: "I just can't see this technique working."

In creating Washinkai, we deliberately pared it down to moves that were effective and entirely realistic. Our rule was: if it worked eighty per cent of the time, we kept it. At the same time, there was a distinct family resemblance to traditional Wado-Ryu. We retained the relatively high stances for speed and ease of movement. At our core, we

Washinkai Karate National Championships in 1979, Bill Smith in action with the katana

Trophy Winners (l to r) John Brock, Joe John, Mustafa el Omari, 1979

continued to observe Ohtsuka's ruling principle – based on ju-jitsu and traditional budo – of using fast evasion and response to turn the opponent's energy against himself, not fighting force with force. In creating Washinkai, I believe we were true to Sensei Ohtsuka's beliefs and guiding principles. We were following a way that seemed natural and right in our own lives and fitted well in our time and culture. That short meeting with Ohtsuka at the Judokan was, in retrospect, the inspiration for the new path. Washinkai is an extension of the philosophy and teachings of the Wado-Ryu founder.

An outsider watching any good karate class should see the same three phases of learning in almost every training session:

1. Kihon: basic techniques – punching, kicking, blocking and striking.
2. Kata: dance-like forms or patterns of movement designed to practise defensive combinations against imaginary opponents.
3. Kumite: karate's equivalent of sparring in boxing.

With Washinkai, the basic kihon retain many of the same techniques you might have seen in a dojo in Japan nearly a hundred years ago. From beginner to black belt, everyone practises blocking and striking with almost every part of the body, repeating these fundamental techniques over and over again, moving in straight lines up and down the length of the dojo. The endless repetition helps to build up a disciplined, fast response to any aggressive situation, for in the real world attack can come without warning and almost certainly without thinking time. We train to develop an automatic reaction to any threat that comes our way. The karate-ka has a split second decision to understand the attack and react to it proportionately. We condition ourselves to have such a reaction, to maintain constant awareness – but relaxed awareness. In Washinkai, speed of movement and balance are crucial and we encourage students to practise staying completely relaxed right up to the final moment of impact: not always an easy thing to do if an attacker is bearing down on you with the clear and obvious intention of doing you harm.

In kihon, if you can transmit as much power with control to the target without wasting energy, then you have grasped the fundamentals of karate. You want minimum effort with maximum effect. You aim for punches, strikes and kicks that have force and energy, but all the while maintaining posture, balance and stability. There should be no wasted energy at all. Control and balance lie at the heart of karate.

With Washinkai, I wanted kata to be more inclusive. They include all the traditional Wado-Ryu forms along with others from different karate styles and two new kata created by me. During my searching period, I realised there were a lot more kata than I'd been taught. At that time, Shotokan and Goju-Ryu katas were winning everything in competition. We immediately adopted some kata from Goju-Ryu, Shito-Ryu and Shotokan.

Some of the kata still carry the names of Chinese diplomats who served in the island of Okinawa – the true home of modern karate – more than two centuries ago. Most of the forms can trace their origin to a historical period when Japanese feudal invaders banned martial arts. Ordinary Okinawans disguised their training routines as dance moves. They would have been executed by the occupying Samurai if discovered, one of the reasons why early Okinawan martial arts were practised in secret.

Where Washinkai does break strongly from tradition is in kumite drills, or practising combat. In all styles, karate students work in pairs to practise pre-arranged defences against attack. Many simple pairs involve blocking or evading a single kick, punch or strike and then responding with one retaliatory technique. This simple routine of evasion and response is a common rhythm in all martial arts training, including tai-chi and kung-Fu. Pair work is designed to give the student a learned toolkit of potential responses to attack. In developing Washinkai, we made the pairs techniques much faster and more realistic, cutting out the archaic intermediate steps of Wado-Ryu that would prove useless and slow on the street. Our grading syllabus now includes a long list of Ohyo Gumite, or advanced pre-arranged pair routines with multiple moves, most of which are new and exclusive to the Washinkai style of karate.

Once this new style was established, we went on the road and did a great deal of tournament work to show established karate followers why we were different. We had to prove our worth. We were tested in competition. In these early years, the syllabus caused a bit of a sensation because it was completely different. More than thirty-five years later, Washinkai has been kept together by the same values we set out to establish in 1977-78. Our

No holds barred: Washinkai national competitionin 1986. Austin Okoye (who used to have Frank Bruno as his sparring partner in his boxing days) against Basil Fraser.

karate was realistic, effective and honest. The techniques worked against an unarmed attacker. Our door was open to everyone. From those first days, there has been no distinction on the basis of colour, social status or background. We have no race or class barriers. Founded in a decade when money talked and corruption was too widespread, it was a relief to get back to honest karate. No one can jump a grading and no one can buy a black belt. Success takes time and commitment. Whether or not you are a natural athlete, the biggest battle is a mental one. The toughest fight is always against yourself and your own mind.

Washinkai summer gasshuku at Port
Regis in Dorset in 1986

chapter 7
WAY OF THE EMPTY HAND

和
心
会

The word 'karate' – usually translated as empty hand – is not simple to define.

Karate as we know it was born in the island of Okinawa, grew to maturity in Japan, but had its ancestral roots and influences very firmly in China. When the Okinawans began practising their secret art of self-defence in the shadow of invading Japanese overlords, it was called To-te jutsu: 'To' being the character for 'China'; 'Te' meaning 'hand'; and 'jutsu' meaning 'art'. So the original name of To-te jutsu meant 'Art of China hand', signifying its largely Chinese influence and inspiration.

This new martial art moved to the Japanese mainland in the early 20th Century, but at that time there was a strong anti-China feeling among the ruling elite in Japan. The authorities in Tokyo simply rewrote history to bring Okinawan-hand – this Art of China hand – within the classical Japanese warrior tradition of budo. They wanted a name that fitted better with the nationalistic prejudices of the time. So it was renamed 'karate', or empty hand. In the Japanese language, the ideogram for China can also mean 'empty'.

However, 'empty hand' can still have several levels of meaning. The traditional translation is that karate is the art or "way" of unarmed self-defence. Its follower is empty handed, or without weapons, in the face of attack. But 'kara' also suggests the spiritual meaning of empty as void or nothingness, which gives us the thought-provoking idea of a defending hand emanating from 'nothingness'. This points to the concept of mushin or 'no mind' that the karate-ka seeks to achieve during meditation and ultimately during the act of fighting – the idea of being able to focus intensely without distraction on the immediate threat and response, living and acting completely in the moment even in the midst of violence.

The organisation that I set up to practise the Washinkai

style of karate is called the British Traditional Karate Association (BTKA). We always seek to maintain traditional values, purposes and methods while also being highly realistic in our training and following a practice in line with modern safety standards. So the BTKA definition of karate goes something like this: the art and science of unarmed self-defence, which leads to a healthier body, mind and spirit. The discipline of constantly practising kihon (basic techniques), kata (form) and kumite (combat drills) develops physical health, self-control and self-confidence as well as a greater understanding of self and others. It strengthens the mind, heart and spirit as well as the body.

Today, the idea of 'empty hand' strikes a note of recognition among most people. Every human being at some time experiences what it is like to stand fearful, alone and empty handed in the face of an aggressive, violent world. The art of karate can help you face up to your fears and find a more confident way to respond to aggression. As the Buddhist monk and peace campaigner Thich Nhat Han says: "Violence is never far." We may not be able to change the world, but we can always learn how to respond better to its endless and often violent challenges.

chapter 8
KARATE HISTORY: THE EARLY YEARS

和心会

Instructors' training group in 1978. On Chris Thompson's left in the back row is Colin Inwood, one of the co-founders of Washinkai Karate.

From very early in my karate career, I realised that if I was to have any credibility at all, then I had to know not only what I was teaching, but why. Many of the Japanese teachers in the 1970s did not understand the background to their techniques or the broader history of karate. I studied Japanese history and read everything I could get my hands on about karate. At the time, it was a revelation to me to learn that so much of Japanese culture was influenced by China. The more you look at karate techniques now, the more you see a Chinese influence.

Documented evidence of systematic fighting can be traced back thousands of years. The Egyptians carved hieroglyphs into the walls of the pyramids depicting fighting scenes. A systematic form of unarmed combat was used in the early Greek Olympic Games, when fights often resulted in death. China's advanced civilization also had a systematic form of unarmed fighting while the rest of the known world still lived in caves. And it is in China, and the story of the Shaolin Temple, that we find the first roots of karate.

The Indian Buddhist monk we know as Bodhidharma (or Daruma in Japanese) – usually credited with being the founder of Zen Buddhism – is said to have travelled from India to China between 530 and 540 AD. According to the story handed down over successive generations, he settled in the Shaolin Temple and introduced a series of training exercises for the existing monks, whose lifestyles had left them unfit and grossly overweight. Today, these exercises would be classed as kung-fu, or wushu, and they are the foundation of modern karate.

The island of Okinawa emerged as the perfect place politically and geographically to nurture the growth of karate, lying as it does half way between China and mainland Japan. Throughout the centuries, the island's loyalties have been divided between Japan and China, both of which tried to colonise it. Okinawa's location also made it an important trading post for many countries of the Far East, a neutral port for nations that were unable to trade with each other because of war or political upheaval.

"Okinawa emerged as the perfect place politcally and geographically to nuture the growth of karate."

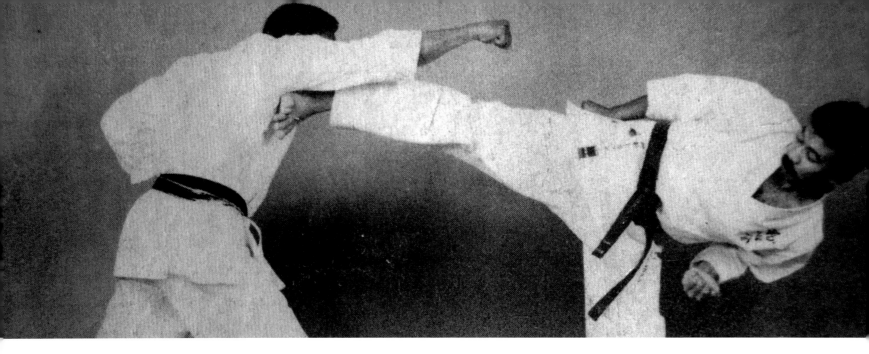

The island became a haven for seamen of many different cultures who, by the very nature of their life and work, were extremely tough and hardened men. They regularly exchanged their own peculiar fighting methods with one another in a friendly way, not least while drinking, but it was not uncommon for the techniques to be exchanged in real combat. The Okinawans used all this invaluable knowledge to form their own eclectic fighting system.

In the 15th and 16th Centuries, Chinese military attaches were based in Okinawa, a reflection of the strong ties between the two countries. In the early 17th Century, the feudal Satsuma clan of Japan invaded Okinawa, quickly forcing the islanders to surrender to their rule. Okinawa was now in effect a colony under the direct rule of the

Sensei Thompson demostrating Washinkai technqiues for Combat Magazine in the 1980s with Roy Gould.

Japanese. The daily life of the Okinawans remained little changed, but all weapons were now confiscated, making the islanders totally subservient. Confiscation of weapons had also taken place earlier in Okinawan history (in 1429) when the king insisted that his people should be motivated by education rather than traditional combat. Only high-ranking government officials and officers were permitted to carry weapons. (See also my first book Essentials of Wado-Ryu Karate, first published in 1988.)

Even though Japan now controlled Okinawa, the islands did not sever their links with the Chinese. Several Chinese military attaches were still permitted to live on the island and they secretly taught the Okinawans Chinese forms of self-defence. This was called 'chuan fa', or Chinese 'fist

way'. The Chinese helped the Okinawans to merge their primitive native forms of self-defence with a much more formalized style of unarmed combat. The fighting system which the Okinawans developed themselves used all parts of their bodies and was generally known as 'Okinawan te' or 'tode'. Despite the secrecy shrouding tode, many began to study the art at an early age, learning from immediate family or very close friends.

The three main towns on Okinawa – Shuri, Tomari and Naha –created their own particular forms of Okinawan te. This led to the use of the phrases we hear often today: Shuri-te, Tomari-te and Naha-te. Shuri-te became Shorin-Ryu, concentrating on faster execution of techniques with emphasis on speed rather than strength. Over the centuries, via visiting Chinese military attaches, monks, seamen and traders, a primitive form of indigenous Okinawan unarmed fighting evolved.

At the beginning of the 20th Century, when the Russo-Japan war was in progress, Japan conscripted heavily from Okinawa. An extremely alert Japanese army doctor noticed that many of these recruits were much fitter and stronger than their counterparts from the Japanese mainland. Investigation revealed these strong conscripts had been practising Okinawan te, so Japanese officials ordered that this early form of karate be included in physical education classes in all Okinawan schools.

They could see the military advantages of such a system, which could be used to condition future soldiers. Eventually, this te became known as 'karate-jutsu', the ideogram of which means 'Chinese hand art'.
When Crown Prince Hirohito saw a demonstration of karate-jutsu during a tour of Okinawa, he was so impressed he included the event in his formal report to the Japanese government. The Ministry of Education then invited an Okinawan expert on karate-jutsu to visit Japan.

The person chosen was Gichin Funakoshi, not because the Okinawans believed he was the best exponent of the art of te, but because he was a primary school teacher and spoke good Japanese. He also came from a good family background. That was essential to give him social credibility among the Japanese hierarchy.

Funakoshi had, in fact, also visited Japan five years before, hoping to introduce karate to the mainland then. He gave a demonstration of Okinawan te to officials from the upper classes and aristocracy, mostly descendants of traditional samurai families. They had dismissed this new karate as no more than a set of drills for street fighting without weapons, fit only for the lower classes – plebeian fighting! The aristocracy believed then that any form of combat that did not use the sword was inferior. The Japanese were also reluctant to accept any type of combat that had not developed directly on the mainland. If it came from Okinawa, it was automatically seen as inferior.

But when Funakoshi returned in 1922, his display was open to the public at a sports festival in Tokyo. Both Funakoshi and his karate-jutsu proved an immediate success. Before long, karate grew in popularity among young Japanese, especially university students. Funakoshi quickly struck up a relationship with Jigoro Kano, the founder of modern-day judo. After many discussions, Funakoshi adopted a style of uniform, or gi, very similar to that worn by the exponents of judo. He also adopted Kano's system of awarding black belts (dan) to his senior students after a formal assessment. This was to prove invaluable. It was one of the requirements set out by the organisation for controlling martial arts, the Dai Nippon Butokukai.

In 1931, karate was accepted as a martial art – under the strict stipulation that certain conditions were met: the word 'karate' was written in Japanese characters and not Chinese; karate schools adopted a standard uniform as well as the black belt system; and a form of tournament was held regularly. It would be wrong to credit Gichin Funakoshi alone with the rapid proliferation of karate in Japan. Many skilled founding fathers influenced the formation of karate and shared in promoting its growth. But from the traditionalist point of view, Funakoshi must be considered the father of Japanese karate-do. He was responsible for making many important innovations to karate-jutsu and he brought this Okinawan art to the Japanese and, later, to a wider western world.

In 1933, Funakoshi changed the concept of 'kara', which was originally written with the Chinese ideogram meaning 'China hand', and substituted another character for 'kara' which signified 'void' or 'empty'. Two years later, Funakoshi discarded the world 'jutsu' in favour of the word 'do' (the way of). Thus, karate-do (as in ju-do and aiki-do) was born in Japan.

Funakoshi established a central dojo or training hall in Tokyo in 1936. He called his dojo 'Shotokan', a name thrust upon him by his students. The ideogram for the prefix 'shoto' was Funakoshi's pen name as a calligrapher, his nick-name. The 'kan' ideogram meant hall. This was to be the honbu or headquarters of his karate organisation, Shotokan, now the most widely practised style of karate across the world.

World War II saw karate-do become officially recognised as a valuable part of the training of the Japanese military, both soldiers and sailors. Mass participation of Japan's

Washinkai Instructor Roy Gould in competition in the mid-1980s

young men resulted in the rapid growth of new unarmed karate techniques. Even after Japan's defeat in the war, when most martial arts were prohibited as they were thought to foster militarism, the karate system continued to flourish. Just as Okinawans practised their te in secret after being invaded by the Satsuma clan, the Japanese now practised their karate-do in hidden forms of training until the ban on martial arts was lifted in 1952.

By the early 1950s, the technical standard of karate-do had increased tremendously. The styles of karate that had been established before the outbreak of World War II now began to flourish and a syllabus was developed for all the various styles now operating. Senior experts of several ryu (schools) established a national body for the new martial arts schools to ensure high standards. This in turn meant far greater numbers of high school and university students entered competitions, making karate an art of both popular appeal and national importance.

Many traditionalists in Okinawa were angered by Funakoshi's change in the meaning of karate to signify empty hand or unarmed fighting. The original Okinawan systems on which karate was based always included the use of specific weapons: bo (a six-foot staff), nunchuku (rice flails), tonfa (rice-grinding flails), sai (large metal pronged forks), kama (sickles) and tekko (metal knuckle dusters). Funakoshi clarified the apparent paradox and gained much support from his fellow Okinawans by declaring that the use of the ideogram 'empty' was based on the concept of unselfishness. Thus, the emptiness suggested by the newly chosen character referred to the state of rendering oneself ego-less. Funakoshi stressed that he taught karate as an exercise for the mind and body that built personal character.

It was during the American armed forces' occupation of Japan after World War II that Westerners gained their first sight of karate-do. Many US servicemen, especially those from the Strategic Air Command, were fascinated by the exercises and drills carried out by the Japanese. The American soldiers wanted to learn karate. The Japanese karate masters hated both the Americans and the idea of teaching occupying soldiers. But they feared that if they closed their doors against the gaijin (Westerners), then the dojos would be closed, leading to loss of income and the marginalisation of karate-do. Once accepted by the Japanese, the US servicemen were taught the finer points of karate-do, making it possible for the knowledge to be spread to the West when the Americans returned home.

Karate was introduced to the Americans in the early 1950s. The Japanese masters quickly grasped the benefits of seeing their arts spread across the world, both in influence and wealth. They wanted to see karate flourish internationally. With Japanese and American trade expanding rapidly after the war, many senior Japanese karate-ka visited the United States and some settled there permanently. Today, every style of Japanese karate has a school somewhere in the US, and practitioners number many thousands.

The Frenchman Henri Plee is credited with introducing karate to Europe in 1957. He was also the first person to bring a Japanese karate expert to Europe. Karate was then introduced to Britain by Vernon Bell, who was one of Plee's students. Bell later invited Japanese teachers to the United Kingdom, including Sensei Hirokazu Kanazawa, the legendary master of Shotokan karate. By the mid-1960s, the demand for karate was so great worldwide that many Japanese karate-ka were invited to teach permanently in countries across the Western World. They settled in the West and brought with them every style of karate, especially Shotokan, Wado-Ryu, Goju-Ryu and Shito-Ryu.

Today, it seems almost every country in the world has at least one karate club. In the past fifty years, the popularity of this martial art has attracted millions of people from every walk of life. Funakoshi could never have dreamt that his beloved art would leave his small island of Okinawa and be studied and taught by people of every race.

chapter 9
DIFFERENT STYLES & WHAT THEY OFFER

和
心
会

The fact that I started out studying Wado-Ryu karate was not a conscious choice on my part, more an accident of time and place. It just happened to be the style taught at the Judokan when I arrived there. Today, there are hundreds of karate styles around the world, but the vast majority can trace their roots back to the handful of Okinawan pioneers who decided to share their knowledge with the rest of the world in the first half of the 20th Century.

Gichin Funakoshi was not the only Okinawan to bring karate to mainland Japan. Many of his compatriots whose roots and tutors were different from those of Funakoshi were also responsible for developing the martial art in Japan. Among them were Chojun Miyagi (1888-1953), who introduced the style of Goju-Ryu karate, and Kenwa

Mabuni (1888-1952), who brought Shito-Ryu to the mainland. Those who were fortunate enough to stay and prosper have left their mark on the world of karate-do.

However, many of the Okinawans who brought their karate to Japan were not openly accepted. Some of them also found it hard to settle into the Japanese way of life and decided to return home. One important example was Kanban Uechi (1877-1948). He had studied martial arts in China at the end of the 19th Century and stayed in China for around thirteen years before returning to Okinawa. In 1924, Uechi went to Japan to teach and by 1940 he had named his method Uechi-Ryu karate. His style never gained the popularity of Funakoshi's, Miyagi's or Mabuni's and he returned to Okinawa in 1947. It was only after his death a year later that Uechi-Ryu became very popular in his native Okinawa. Kanban Uechi's son continued to teach the style after his father's death, but it never grew at the rate Kanban Uechi wanted.

Shotokan karate

Gichin Funakoshi (1868-1957), already acknowledged as the founder of modern karate, was reluctant to call his style a school, or ryu – he simply labelled it karate-do. His teachings in the 1930s differed greatly from his contemporaries in Okinawa and from the way he himself was taught. He had a profound effect on all his students and placed much emphasis upon their mental awareness, alongside physical prowess.

The Shotokan we are familiar with today can be credited more to Funakoshi's third son, who was affectionately called Giko. He – just like the Wado-Ryu founder Hironori

Ohtsuka – believed in applying karate techniques in actual free fighting. As with all young men of that generation, he wanted to test his skills on a real opponent. By 1936, when Funakoshi established his Shotokan school of karate in Tokyo, he was already sixty-eight years old. Even though he had a tremendous following, a great burden and responsibility was placed upon his son. The young Funakoshi's style was very different to that of his father. Gichin Funakoshi had always adopted high stances; those of his son were much lower, as in Shotokan today. His son also used full leg extension techniques such as mawashigeri (roundhouse kick) and yoko-geri (side kick), which he is credited with introducing to karate. The kata of Shotokan are numerous and some even have derivations which reflect the older Funakoshi's teachings. Today, Shotokan is the style of karate most practised throughout the world.

Wado-Ryu (a Japanese style of karate)

The founder of Wado-Ryu karate, Hironori Ohtsuka (1892-1982) – who had such an important impact on my own future when I met him at the Judokan – was born in Shimodate City, Ibaraki prefecture, Japan. By the time he was six years old, he had already started training ju-jitsu, studying under his maternal great-uncle. When he entered middle school at the age of thirteen he started to study Shindo Yoshin-Ryu ju-jitsu under Tatsusabaro Nakayama. These studies with Nakayama continued throughout his education at Waseda University, resulting in Ohtsuka being awarded his menkyo (licence-level proficiency) in Shindo Yoshin-Ryu under Nakayama in 1921.

The following year, Ohtsuka heard of a karate demonstration given by Gichin Funakoshi in Tokyo and was determined to meet him. Throughout his studies of ju-jitsu, Ohtsuka had always sought to learn from other competing styles of ju-jitsu, trying to visit as many different dojo as possible. When karate arrived in mainland Japan, he could not contain his excitement at the advent of a completely new, weapon-less martial art.

He met Funakoshi at his residence, a boarding house for Okinawan students. They talked for several hours discussing their different interpretations of the martial arts and by the end of that evening Funakoshi had agreed to accept Ohtsuka as a student of his karate jutsu. Ohtsuka started training with Funakoshi immediately and his enthusiasm and martial arts background meant that he quickly grasped the physical techniques that he was being taught. In just over a year, he had studied and knew the movements of every single kata that Funakoshi had taught him. At that time, kata was the only aspect of karate that Funakoshi taught. Throughout this period,

Ohtsuka did not stop training in ju-jitsu and began to incorporate this into his karate. In April 1924 at the age of thirty-one, Ohtsuka was graded black belt by Funakoshi, so becoming one of the first Japanese black belts in karate. The continued devotion of Ohtsuka to both karate and ju-jitsu meant he quickly became not only Funakoshi's assistant instructor but also Shihan (Grand Master) of Shindo Yoshin-Ryu. He also began to train with other famous martial artists such as Kenwa Mabuni, founder of the Shito-Ryu style and Choki Motobu, famed as a fighter in karate. Then Ohtsuka began teaching at Tokyo University and his methods began to conflict with those of Funakoshi. Ohtsuka's brand of karate incorporated his ju-jitsu techniques, enabling his students to practise free sparring. This was not to Funakoshi's liking. Funakoshi felt that actual sparring, jissen, was far too dangerous and would immediately result in the death of one of the participants. Ohtsuka believed that students could use techniques in free fighting without severe injury so long as there were specific guidance and rules. The two men went their separate ways and Ohtuska set up his own style of karate, to be called Wado-Ryu. The split had become inevitable.

Goju-Ryu karate

Goju-Ryu, meaning 'hard-soft school' was founded by the Okinawan Chojun Miyagi, one of the few students of the great Kannryo Higoanna, a naha-te karate instructor. Miyagi studied with Higoanna until his death in 1915 and then travelled to China to learn various forms of wushu, the Chinese martial art. When he returned to Okinawa, he merged his wushu teachings (soft) with his naha-te teachings (hard). In this context, soft means using evasive techniques to use an opponent's attacking energy against himself and hard refers to a more confrontational, meet-force-with-force style of karate. He took the name Goju from a passage in the Bubishi, a handwritten book passed down over several hundred years from one generation of martial artists to the next. Like other Okinawans who had become experts in martial arts, Miyagi was invited to Japan to teach his Goju style of karate. He travelled to Kyoto and other cities in southern Japan, but found himself extremely homesick. Gogen Yamaguchi was one of his last Japanese disciples and, before he returned to Okinawa, Miyagi passed Yamaguchi the mantle, letting him become his senior disciple in Japan. Yamaguchi, in turn, created a different style of Goju. The fundamentals were still there, but he gave it more of a Japanese influence. Today, we have two forms of Goju-Ryu karate: Goju-Ryu and Goju-Kai. Yamaguchi placed a great deal of emphasis on internal strength. Both forms of Goju are well represented worldwide.

Shito-Ryu karate

The founder of Shito-Ryu was Kenwa Mabuni (1889-1952), an Okinawan who also had as an instructor Kannryo Higoanna – the same man who had instructed Miyagi and Anko Itosu, one of Funakoshi's instructors. This gave Mabuni a chance to practise all three of the Okinawan styles of karate: naha-te, shuri-te and tomari-te. As a close friend of Miyagi, Mabuni also travelled to China with him to study the Chinese wushu forms. With such a great amassed amount of knowledge, Mabuni created a style based on more than sixty kata and he called it Hankoryu. He eventually changed the name to Shito-Ryu, which was an amalgamation of the two great original instructors who had taught him: Itosu and Higoanna. Mabuni travelled to Japan in the late 1920s and settled in the southern area of the country near Osaka, where he taught his Shito-Ryu. It is very popular in Japan and is also highly popular on the tournament circuit all around the world.

Kyokushinkai karate

Kyokushinkai was founded by Matsutatsu (Mas) Oyama (1923-1994). Even though it is not one of the four original karate styles of Japan, it is still popular in Japan and across the world.

Mas Oyama was born in Korea and later naturalized as Japanese. His Kyokushinkai karate, or 'school of ultimate truth', is as close to combat as one could get. Its concept of ikkken hisatsu (one punch, one kick technique) to stop an opponent are the foundation of the style. This is why it immediately became very popular with the Japanese. Oyama was influenced by both Funakoshi of

Shotokan and by Yamaguchi of Goju-Kai, but found that neither of these styles could convey the true combative spirit he was searching for. After a period of self-imposed isolation away from the city and the limelight, Oyama re-emerged to demonstrate his own style of karate by fighting bulls bare handed, successfully killing three, each with a single blow. This gave him immediate popularity. Having a cartoon strip in a national magazine also highlighted his fame. At one stage, his style was one of the fastest growing karate schools in the world. Since his death, however, the Kyokushinkai organisation has declined, although the style is still practised.

Its popularity is due to the dynamic actions of the techniques and it appeals to spectators in the same way that gladiators in the Coliseum appealed to the Romans. Towards the end of his life, Oyama spent much of his time organising tournaments that relied on an opponent being knocked down to determine the winner. This made it easy for spectators to see who had won and who had lost, not always the case in competitions involving other styles. Kyokushinkai proudly boasts of being extremely hard and unrelenting in its training. It is full-contact karate in every sense.

chapter 10
WAR CRIMES & THE VALUES OF KARATE

和心会

Every war has its atrocities, on all sides. But it is little known in the West, even today, that one of the early Japanese masters and teachers of karate was regarded as a war criminal by many of the American forces who became the occupying power in Japan at the end of the Second World War.

The allegation against this particular karate master – disputed, of course, by his own followers – is that during the war he had Allied prisoners of war tied down so he could practise karate techniques on them. He used prisoners who couldn't fight back and were often weak and close to death in a series of live training routines to see how effective his karate proved to be in real life, if such experiments can ever be described as real life. He died at home in Tokyo of natural causes in 1945.

In acting as he did, this sensei may have been following the example of traditional Samurai warriors who had been known to test their swords on living prisoners or on commoners of inferior rank who offended them in some way, real or imagined. Historically, Samurai were often mercenary bully boys enforcing feudalism with the sword rather than the romantic warrior heroes we think of today. They believed that defeat in battle was shameful.

They had no tolerance of weakness. The militaristic mind of many of the Japanese forces in the Second World War inherited this historic intolerance of anything they perceived as weakness. To Western eyes and values, the Japanese of the Second World War era could seem a barbaric and cruel race, which is one reason why friends of my parents reacted so strongly when I took up karate as a teenager.

Today, how do these alleged war crimes fit with the constant mantra heard in dojo around the world that respect for self and others lies at the heart of karate?

In The Twenty Guiding Principles of Karate, Gichin Funakoshi is quoted as saying that unless all martial arts are practised with a feeling of reverence and respect, they are simply forms of violence. "Karate is a martial art in which the hands and feet are like swords, and it must not be used unjustly or improperly. Karate practitioners must stand on the side of justice at all times and only in situations where there is no other choice should their power find expression through the use of their hands and feet as weapons." In the end, it was these values of respect for justice and humanity expressed and practised by Funakoshi that guided the growth of karate in the West.

Today, the practical reality is that Japan is no longer the sole gatekeeper of karate's values. Immediately after the Second World War, soldiers from the US Strategic Air Command became interested in Japanese history and in traditional martial arts. They wanted to learn this magical art of karate. The Japanese masters who founded karate hated the Americans, but realised if they refused to teach them, then the occupying US forces would simply shut down all the dojo. Not only did these American soldiers take karate home with them to the West, but the Japanese founders of karate saw the opportunity to expand the influence of their cherished martial arts around the world and rebuild their lives and organisations financially after the devastation of the atomic bomb attacks on Hiroshima and Nagasaki. At the same time, karate and other martial arts started to lose their magic for new generations of young people in Japan, who turned to the American imports of baseball and basketball for leisure instead of traditional dojo.

The core values of karate can only ever be as good as the people who teach and practise in dojo around the world. Having taught many thousands of students over more than forty years, my own experience is that something exceptional happens to students who train hard and consistently in martial arts. Karate-ka who confront their own fears and physical and mental limitations – and let's face it, we all have these limitations – learn to stand a little taller in life. They look the world squarely in the eye and develop a new confidence and respect for themselves. Once an individual learns self-respect, then it is a short journey to understanding the need for respect for others as a core value in life. After respect comes a natural humility, born of the sure and certain knowledge that someone better, faster and stronger can always be waiting round the next corner.

The point is that these core values can never be imposed from above by the rules of any organisation. They must and do grow from within each individual during the constant training that karate and all martial arts demand. It is a gift, a magical process. And it is available to you whether you're seven or seventy. The desire to walk into the dojo and be better today than you were yesterday is a positive, energetic force in life. It keeps you fit and young in mind, heart and body.

chapter 11
THE WASHINKAI FAMILY

和心会

Washinkai karate has followers all over the world. Today our clubs are spread across southern England, and we have dojo in Northern Ireland, Spain and Scandinavia. At various stages in the last forty years, Washinkai has also been practised in the United States, Hong Kong and Japan. Every summer, these club members gather from every point of the compass for a week-long training camp in Dorset. It has a real family atmosphere. This has been a constant theme in all my work – the idea of karate as a family. Unlike most other sports and leisure pursuits, karate allows families to train together and even compete together. That bond is one of the things that makes Washinkai special. A few years ago, a former West Country instructor, Luci Harris, put it like this: "When families do train together, I think we find something that is often lost in modern life – a time and place for parents and children to get together and enjoy each other, to watch and celebrate each other's successes. It's an opportunity to appreciate how hard we have tried or worked to reach that always elusive next step. It's also a chance to watch each other grow in years, in confidence and in character. And training together gives us the humility just to realise we are all human and we all make mistakes sometimes." Crucially, says Luci, karate is one family we choose for ourselves. "In the dojo, we see each other at our strongest, weakest and most vulnerable. Yet no one is afraid. The word 'family' means strength in Washinkai. Together we are much stronger than we can ever be on our own."

In Dorset, the Gawler family from Milborne Port have been involved in karate for much of their lives. Father Pat and son James are now both Third Dan black belts and daughter Emma is also a Third Dan black belt. They say Washinkai feels like home. Emma Gawler tells their story: "Over the years, dad, James and I had practised at various karate clubs, but when they joined Washinkai school commitments meant I didn't have the time to carry on.

"As I saw them progress through the grades and reach Shodan and Nidan, I must say I felt quite disappointed I had given up. Then I realised just how much I regretted

The Gawler Karate family from Dorset: James, Emma and father Pat.

that. So I took up karate again and it was best decision I've made in a very long time!"

"The feeling of unity between the three of us since I restarted is amazing. I feel so much more connected to my family again. For us, karate is more than just a hobby. It's become part of our life. It doesn't stop when we leave the dojo. We're always discussing different aspects at home, sharing our opinions and thoughts on different things: the lessons, courses, techniques ... everything and anything you could possibly think of. I don't think I have spoken so much and so often to dad in years. Now I almost see the whole karate club as a family, not just James and dad. The one thing I noticed when I first set foot in the dojo was the feeling of community ... the feeling that everyone looks out

"If you need help, there is always someone to turn to. Nobody ever turns their back on you ."

for one another, everyone is part of something bigger. If you need help, there is always someone to turn to. Nobody ever turns their back on you. They always offer support and encouragement. The feeling of being an important aspect of a team is overwhelming. When it comes down to it, isn't that really what a family is – people who stick together no matter what and look out for one another, support and encourage one another to improve?

"When you train as a family, what happens outside of the dojo is significant: the increased communication, the feeling of being part of something together. Not only does karate keep us all fit and healthy, it has given us a bigger goal in our lives, something to always aim for, a constant way to improve ourselves. I think that's important for any family."

The Gawler family's instructor, Paul Hacker (5th Dan), has been teaching martial arts professionally for more than ten years and is now based at the Honbu, a purpose built dojo created out of the ruins of an abandoned motor repair garage in Wincanton, Somerset. As well as running his own club at the Honbu, Paul teaches at a series of leading schools in the West Country, including Millfield, the specialist sports school. He has seen successive generations of children and students take up karate. "You share a lot of your life with your friends and students in the dojo. Often, you can talk to them in ways you can't talk to your own family. For example, I met Jason Brown (now Fourth Dan) when he was twelve and we were still training at the old Methodist Hall up the street. He's twenty-nine now. I have watched him grow up through school, university and on to work in oil rigs. These days, he chooses to come back to the Honbu as often as he can to train with all his old friends. It's just the same with his boyhood school friend Alex Thick, who joined the club when he was thirteen and is now a successful businessman based in Portsmouth. He returns whenever he can. It's like a family. Another student who grew up in our club and now lives in Plymouth says, perhaps rather indiscreetly: 'These days, the only reason I come home is for karate.'

"A lot of children are extremely unconfident when they first start training. It's great to see them blossom. The

Sensei Thompson with a young Paul Hacker, now 5th Dan Black Belt and a professional instructor at the Honbu Dojo in Somerset.

important thing is, we're not there to judge you. We'll help you through. At grading exams, two people doing the same belt may be very different in talent and technique, but as long as I can see they're doing the best they possibly can, then that is all I can ever ask. Of course, there is another important way in which karate is like a family. I am now part of a community of fellow karate-ka. If I phone them in the middle of the night and say I'm in trouble, then they will come and help -- without question. That is family in a very real and special sense. It's also quite rare, I think. "

Dave Martin, the head of Washinkai Karate Ireland, puts it another way. "Like all good family members, they are not there all the time, but they ARE there when it matters." Dave started training in the mid-1970s in Hampshire with

Tatsuo Suzuki's Wado Ryu organisation and despite the practical difficulties of work commitments and a spell of several years living in the Netherlands, karate became a pillar of his life. When Dave was teaching martial arts in Warwick, his future wife Michele joined his class as a beginner. After they married, they moved to Michele's home town of Omagh in Northern Ireland to start a family. Now Dave (6th Dan) and Michele (5th Dan) run clubs in Enniskillen, Omagh and Irvinestown. Their three children aged 15, 13 and nine have taken up karate, train alongside mum and dad and all are moving up through the ranks. "Of course we train together," says Dave, "otherwise it would be an empty experience. I expect my children to reach black belt! We also play music together and hang out on the boat together and enjoy each other's company. We all have individual activities, but doing things together is what makes our family work. Karate is an ideal vehicle for our development, both personal and as a team. While we try to teach children about life, they teach us what life is all about. I am an independent person but value the back-up and support of family and friends. I don't need to be part of Washinkai, but I choose to be and have never regretted that decision. Karate has been the cornerstone of my life. It has sometimes been a difficult mistress, but it has never let me down."

Sensei Dave Martin (6th Dan), head of Washinkai Karate in Ireland

Asked whether he and his wife ever argue about karate,

167

Ireland

Sensei Martin replied: "I am always right about karate. She is right about everything else." Now that Michele has recently been awarded her 5th Dan black belt, perhaps even that distinction will become less and less clear!

Another family train alongside the Martins: a father and three daughters, the youngest of the children just seven. "Dad studied karate in England when he worked there and renewed his interest after realising he needed exercise for his health. He is head teacher at a primary school and acts as our child protection officer. They are a great asset to the group and really take on board the karate family ethos."

One of the most successful and unusual partnerships in

Sensei Thompson with students of Washinkai Ireland.

Washinkai is the Taylor family. Roy Taylor Senior (5th Dan) heads a network of karate clubs in Surrey and Berkshire. His son Roy Taylor Junior (3rd Dan) – now in his early Thirties – has built up a highly successful career as a film and TV stuntman. Credits include Harry Potter, Bourne Ultimatum, Dark Knight Rises, Hercules, Da Vinci Code, Game of Thrones, Bond movies, War Horse, Pirates of the Caribbean, Flight 93 and the TV series Merlin, Foyle's War, Casualty, Waking the Dead and Safe House

As with so many family partnerships, it was the child who initially sparked the father's interest. "I started when I was seven," says Roy Taylor Jr. "Dad used to take me to lessons and sat there waiting for me … and watching. Then he took up karate himself and joined the seniors' class, so I would be waiting for him. As a child, I never found it embarrassing. It just made sense – he might as well join in. Over the years, I remember practising with my dad, especially at competitions. He would be screaming advice at me, or I would be shouting encouragement to him. It could get a little bit emotional. It was just part of the culture, no longer father and son, but two students training together, just part of the karate brotherhood."

Roy Taylor Jr had dreamed of being a stunt man almost as long as he has practised karate. "One day, dad and I were out in the car and playing a sort of game talking about what

our dream job would be. Dad wanted to be a stunt man, but with a family and three kids to support it was impractical. From that day, I held on to the dream. As a kid, it wasn't the movie stars who were the heroes for me. I admired the stunt men. When I was sixteen and left school, the careers advice people were no help. I just had to work it out for myself." And that's just what he did. For the next nine years, he designed his own programme of education to win entry to the Stunt Register, the essential talent bible of his profession. He went to drama school so he could work as an extra in TV and films and at the same time trained himself in the physical disciplines required of stunt crews: martial arts, riding, trampoline, scuba diving, swimming and rock climbing. He paid his way working the door in pubs and club and also worked as bodyguard.

Although he couldn't know it at the time, it turns out that karate was the greatest gift dad could have given Roy Jr. "It's a great foundation for stunt work: learning how to fall, being able to take a few knocks. And of course, a lot of the bread and butter stuff of stunt work is stage fighting. Rehearsing that is just like doing pairs in Washinkai. Also, in karate you learn confidence, focus, being totally committed, controlling fear and understanding all the different emotions that come up when you are facing someone on the competition mat. The same goes for stunt work. You need a hundred per cent focus. The stunts can

Roy Taylor Jnr uses karate as a professional film stunt actor. Credits include KIck Ass, Safe House and the forthcoming Avengers: Age of Ultron.

171

be life threatening. Learning kata in the karate club is good training for remembering the choreography for a big Hollywood stunt."

In karate, we don't lose touch with our family when they move abroad. I first met my friend Shaz Shahid (6th Dan) in 1980 when he found his way to the Judokan in London, having started martial arts shortly before that with a different style of karate. Not long after receiving his black belt in London, Shaz moved to Hong Kong for ten years to pursue his career as a banker. There, he became Hong Kong national karate champion twice and competed at international level for Hong Kong. Shaz says: "The Far East opened a new chapter in my life. I was faced with new challenges both at work and at karate. After an intensive

Shaz Shahid in action during a recent course at The Honbu, Somerset.

search I found a high standard Goju-Ryu dojo.

"Once they saw my training standard, karate attitude and techniques, my fellow karate-ka in the Far East developed a great respect for Washinkai and Sensei Thompson. Years of studying Goju Ryu in Hong Kong did not change my Washinkai origin. In 1999, I returned to the UK and once again Chris Thompson welcomed the knowledge and techniques I gained from another style. Washinkai never feared other styles. Instead, it welcomed the variety of techniques karate-ka bring from outside as a path to further development. It's this open attitude that makes Washinkai unique."

For all his success in the UK and internationally, Shaz

reminds us – like so many other karate followers who became expert fighters and competitors – that he was never a natural athlete in the beginning of his martial arts career. He had to work hard for each part of his success. "Some people are born with good physique, a sense of speed and a lot of stamina. That's fine, but for me everything I learned was an acquired skill learned through continuous hard training, determination and discipline. Having tried other sports with not much satisfaction and been picked on enough times in school, I decided I needed something more in life. I stumbled on karate. Just by chance I walked into a karate club over thirty years ago and that was a new beginning for me. Eventually, Washinkai became more like a family and a second home."

In my own home today, karate is very much a family affair, with my wife Alison now a 6th Dan black belt and successful martial arts teacher. I always wanted my son James to achieve black belt before going to university and I'm proud to say he has done that. But when I was a young man, my devotion to karate was one of the main reasons my first marriage failed. Right from the beginning, karate had a magnetic attraction for me. I was made for karate and it was made for me. At long last, here was something I loved. I didn't want to know about anything else. Nothing else mattered. I'm sure that is one of the main reasons my first marriage eventually ended in divorce. I married

Chris Thompson's son James during his first-dan black belt grading in 2011

too young. I wasn't a good father as a young man in my twenties. Everything was sacrificed to karate. Most of the decisions I made were geared towards it. I was completely smitten. My first wife Barbara – we met at high school – tolerated my devotion to karate and accepted the situation, but the marriage was doomed. The tenacity and stubbornness you need to devote your life to martial arts made me a bad husband and father first time round and I'm not proud of that, though my parents always believed there is a reason for everything and that disappointments can often transform themselves into a better way of life.

I first met my second wife Alison in 1981 when she turned up at one of my karate classes in Honeywell School in London. She had worked for the Foreign Office and was stationed at the British Embassy in Tehran in the late Seventies when Ayatollah Khomeini came to power. It was in Tehran that she first came across colleagues who practised karate and she decided to give it a try herself when she returned to London. Like so many gifted and expert karate-ka, she didn't feel at all confident or natural as a beginner. "If I'm being honest," says Alison, "I just wanted to keep fit cheaply when I started. I had tried swimming, hockey and netball at school but never felt especially comfortable doing them. But with karate, it quickly became exciting going to classes twice a week. In my first grading for orange belt, I received only a third-class pass – the lowest

rank – and I was really angry with myself. But I kept going, successfully passed my first black belt grading in 1984 and started teaching around that time, too.

"There's no doubt at all in my mind that we are all part of a karate family. I know that in my own teaching, I always feel a complete empathy for the beginner. When I was coming up through the ranks I always had the feeling that other people were better than me, so I know how nervous the new students can be. For me, karate has been a real challenge. It really does demand staying power.

Now I can't imagine not doing it. I'm always striving to do better, and failing most of the time. It's a mental thing, this need to constantly analyse and challenge myself. But

Competitive spirit: a Washinkai referee's course in 1987.

isn't that one of the reasons we do it at all, and one of the great benefits?" As well as teaching at Washinkai clubs around greater London, Alison taught martial arts at five schools in Hampshire, the students usually ranging in age from twelve to nineteen. "They come from a wide range of cultural backgrounds – from the Middle East, China, America, Russia and Poland as well as British-born. Again and again, I see young karate-ka grow into a great sense of achievement and self-esteem. There's a prestige in knowing they could defend themselves if they had to. I see the teacher simply as a wise guide trying to lead out the best in each individual and I suppose that's what it means to be a good parent and to live in a good family."

chapter 12
A SENSE OF BELONGING

Mark Lester hit international fame in the movie Oliver with his portrayal of Oliver Twist.

In the late 1960s, just as I began my own karate career, the child actor Mark Lester became internationally famous for his role as Oliver Twist in the British film Oliver, directed by Carol Reed. He was just ten years old at the time and soon earning a fortune and travelling the world to promote the film, adored both by screaming teenagers and by not-so-young admirers. "I went to places I'd never been to before," he said in an interview in the Independent newspaper around twenty years ago, "America, Japan, Hong Kong. I was picked up at the airport, by-passing customs. That was quite good fun, I suppose. Sometimes it got a bit boring, especially in America, where little old ladies with their blue rinsed hair would come up and grab you by the cheeks and go 'aren't you cute?' My father used to say, 'Well, that's the prices of fame.'"

Mark continued his career with film parts in Run Wild, Run Free, Black Beauty and the Prince and the Pauper. He was thought to be the highest paid child actor in the world, earning up to £100,000 a year – a huge fortune at the time – and still receiving 25 pence a week pocket money from his parents. At the age of eighteen, with access to some of his fortune, he bought a Ferrari and a house in Belgravia, dabbled a little with drugs and lived the life of a fading star in London. "I blew about £70,000 on stupid things, a very expensive car which got written off and nightclubs. I'd always pick up the bill. It's very easy to spend a lot of money in a short space of time, going out. I put it down to an irresponsible 18 year old, which I was at the time, being given a lot of money."

With adulthood, Mark's film career faded and the headlines inevitably changed. He became in the eyes of the British press "Oliver's sad Twist" and "The child star who wanted more and more."

Mark turned to karate to help him find a new way in life and that is when I first met him in London. He practised Washinkai karate with us for ten years or so between the early Eighties and early Nineties, first with my friend Graham Smith in Fulham and also in my own classes at the Judokan. When we spoke just before publication of this book, Mark said he remembered well those personal struggles of the Eighties. "I was at an in-between phase in my life, working as a waiter in my dad's restaurant in Covent Garden and not really sure where the future was going. I used karate to give myself a sense of direction, to find some guidance about what I should do next. About four years into my karate training, I decided I wanted to do something involved with sports injuries."

Mark is now a professional osteopath running a highly successful practice in Cheltenham. "Had it not been for karate, I don't think I would have gone down this path and found my new life. At the time, I didn't know which way to turn. The discipline of karate helped me get a grip on what was really happening in my life. I found a new sense of direction, a feeling of belonging. The karate club was very friendly, like a good family. Then there was also the discipline and the fitness ... that definitely helped me change direction."

Mark went back to school in his late Twenties to study the A-levels he had missed as a child actor and then joined the four-year professional course at the British School of Osteopathy, where he met his first wife Jane. "Looking back over the last twenty years and more, it's clear that I chose the right path and karate undoubtedly helped with that. Practising karate helped me spiritually, physically and emotionally."

chapter 13
CHILDREN IN KARATE

和心会

If there has been a real revolution in karate in the last fifty years, it's in the average age of the students training in dojo up and down the country. When I started practising karate in the late Sixties, children were not allowed in martial arts dojo at all. Today, around three quarters of all karate-ka are children and young teenagers. No professional karate instructor could make a living without them. When I ask these children why they train so hard and what benefits karate brings into their lives, one word comes up again and again: confidence – not only the confidence to stand up to bullies in the playground and on the street, but the belief in themselves to embrace challenges they never before thought possible.

Every year, scores of teenagers take the grading for their

cherished black belt. They are required as part of the exam to send me an essay discussing what difference karate has made in their lives. These extraordinary stories give a humbling insight into the fears and triumphs of these young people. "Throughout my teenage years," said one pint-sized black student, "I struggled with many of the confidence issues that racial minorities of smaller stature would be expected to. I often worried about how I was perceived by those around me and whether I appeared an easy target for verbal abuse, which unfortunately I was from time to time. However, looking back, it is impossible to deny that the more years I put into karate, the less often I would find myself in these situations." Why? Not because this teenager turned into a street fighter – although he did become a strong competitor in karate championships – but because he carried himself with a new aura of confidence, an intangible but very real quality.

"A karate-ka carries himself with pride and dignity even when outside the dojo. The high shoulders and the confident smile that come with the knowledge of how to protect oneself do not make a karate-ka appear an easy target. And when I'm in highly physical situations such as rugby matches or music festivals I never feel anxious because I am secure in my belief that I can keep myself safe."

For women, this sense of safety can be an especially precious thing. "Being a girl, I feel at times we are very vulnerable," says one high school student from Hampshire. "But by doing karate I now feel that I am able to know what to do in a threatening situation, which I hope never happens to me. But karate does give me a peace of mind that my feet would not just be glued to the ground if I were threatened. I would have more knowledge of how to act."

Or more directly, from a teenage girl in Somerset: "Before I started karate, I was bullied a lot about my height and who my friends were. After I joined karate and had passed a couple of gradings, I had gained the confidence to stand up to the bullies and tell them where they could shove their bullying. After that, they left my friends and me alone and haven't come back since."

Again in Hampshire, another girl finds karate training helps with a perennial worry that afflicts all of us at some stage of our lives: fear of the dark, whether real or psychological or spiritual. "I feel like I have acquired an instinctive set of reactions that would stand me in better stead than the average person in a threatening situation. Whilst I hope I never have to use these skills, it has given me the benefit of being a little more confident when it comes to the worries of, for example, walking around a town after dark."

For one teenage boy, training at the Washinkai club in Petersfield, it was not only the confidence C-word that mattered, but also self-control: karate, he said, helped him control his aggression and try harder to understand another person's point of view. "Before I started karate, I was a young shy boy who didn't have many friends. Now after four years of karate, my confidence has grown tremendously. With the increasingly boisterous nature of young teenagers, it was clear to me that knowing and learning a martial art is a valuable tool to defend myself from those certain characters who take the game too far.

"Karate has also helped me to learn to control my anger and realise that arguments don't have to be settled in aggressive fashion, but instead by understanding the other person's side of the story. Karate helps to release and focus your energy rather than misusing it in order to have an unnecessary brawl with someone over a very small problem. This idea of focussing your energy will be very important and useful to me in later life as I have to accept that not everyone will do as I tell them to all the time. I am starting to understand this concept now and instead of getting angry I try and find an easy solution to the problem."

Being in the karate family brought this boy closer to his own mother and father and also helped to increase his sense of self-belief. "As I improved in karate, I started to believe that I am capable of doing most things. I just have to work hard to get them. But this strength is forever encouraging me to push myself to my limits." Karate had also brought his family closer together, he said. "Another benefit I have gained is more support from my family, especially from my mum and dad who have always been there to take me to events and gradings. This has brought me closer to them and also brought them closer to me." As an instructor who has trained many thousands of children over the years, I still smile with satisfaction at the memory of how many young people grow in confidence and self-respect through martial arts.

A Scottish teenage girl whose family moved to Spain and who now trains at the1 Washinkai club in Spain says: "The club, to me, is my extended family. I feel privileged to have been able to go through most of my childhood with it. I remember the first grading I took to get my yellow belt. I was so pleased. I had the biggest smile on my face and from then on I feel that with every belt I got my smile got bigger and bigger.

"At first I didn't like it. In fact, for about six months I was comparing it to my previous [Tae Kwon Do] club and complaining that they didn't do this, that or the other. But slowly I let my guard down (not literally) and realised that here it wasn't all about the fighting and beating each other up. It's the whole essence of how you live."

Another British-born student whose family moved to Spain writes: "When I first started karate I was a five year old boy who had come to live in a foreign country, started a foreign school and soon became the target for bullies. My teacher said she knew it wasn't me that started trouble, but somehow I always got caught finishing it. Soon after I began karate the bullying stopped. I think this was mainly because of the self-confidence I had. It's not the ability to fight that's important, but the capacity to defend myself.

"I have also developed the skill of teaching and team work and am proud to be asked to help teach the younger and lower grades in our class. I have discovered that karate is a constant learning process that enables me to transfer these skills to everyday life and my academic life. At school, I benefit from more energy levels, greater concentration and the skills to finish one task and move on to the next."

Of course, the students have to write these essays before they can be awarded a black belt, so perhaps they have a vested interest in talking up the benefits of karate, but not always. A Somerset teenager writes: "I find myself not that great at karate fighting, so my confidence falters and I just lose the point of competing and drag myself to karate with the attitude of a dog going to the vet. Sometimes I find it quite terrible being dragged along to karate, but eventually fall in and just get on with it and start enjoying it at the end. I thought about quitting a few times, but I remind myself that I am strong because I do karate. It gives me the determination I need to continue with things I find near impossible. For instance, there was once a time when a random boy kept mouthing off towards me, swearing at me, but I knew I had to get back on to my feet and turn around, stare the guy in the eye and let him see that I wasn't afraid. The boy then immediately backed down and scurried off. I felt very proud but also a bit ashamed of myself for succumbing to my strong self."

Of course, competition fighting is not for everyone and no one is ever forced to enter competitions. In fact, a very small percentage of karate-ka actually do so.

A teenager from Somerset who had been studying karate for eight years when he took his black belt grading managed to sum up very succinctly most of the benefits of karate: fitness, self-control, self-defence and self-discipline. "There has been a definite increase in my physical fitness since I began karate. I attend at least two sessions every week for an hour and a half and it is quite a demanding physical sport. We also do monthly half-hour fitness sessions which help me to check that my fitness is at the correct level. Obviously, from learning karate for this amount of time I have learnt a great deal about self-defence. I'm quite confident that I'd be able to get myself out of an emergency if there was no available help. I have developed self-control. I now know how not to damage myself carelessly when using violence. I have also become more confident physically and I have learnt self-discipline. Karate is not easy and you must put a lot of work into it. You have to remember moves, grading syllabuses and practical techniques as well as some of the Japanese language."

In Northern Ireland, a teenage girl student talks about self-respect and respect for others as one of the lasting outcomes of many years of training and hard work. "Standing at the doorway of the dojo in my crisply ironed karate suit with a tightly tied white belt, at ten years old I gazed into the dojo, excited and eager to learn. Seven years later, I stand with a sense of achievement as I now prepare for my first dan grading. Over the years, my journey and commitment to karate training have taught a number of valuable qualities, lessons and an outlook of life. I've had the privilege to mix with people of different ages, background and abilities, all teaching and contributing to my outlook of the study of karate.

"I feel karate has taught me to have both self-respect and respect for others, giving me a sense of confidence that may not come with other types of sports. This sense of confidence has not only developed in karate, but has also contributed to other aspects of my life, allowing me to both be physically and mentally aware and able to defend myself in certain situations. I hope I will never have to use my skills on the street.

"Over the years, karate has taught me the importance of commitment and given me a sense of pride and importance of belonging to a club. It also helps me to deal with the demands of school and the business of home life, as well as giving me both enjoyment and a sense of achievement."

All these students reflect the truth that nothing comes easy in karate, but benefits do come as a result of dedication and hard work and they can last a lifetime. Indeed, karate training can influence your whole path in life. One of my favourite stories comes from a young black belt who wants to become a doctor and talked about karate training in his application to medical school at university. "When called for interview, I was asked why I thought a proficiency in committing violence was an appropriate attribute for a healer. I replied that a proficiency in karate meant that I would be far less likely to panic and inflict harm on a patient during a confrontation, as I am completely aware of the capabilities of my own body and the damage I can inflict. The patience needed to learn and hold karate techniques is transferrable to a future hospital work place

where dealing calmly with rude patients is an everyday occurrence."

He's quite right. I have spent quite a large part of my career in martial arts teaching doctors, nurses and other medical staff to take care of themselves in confrontational situations at work, but that is another story ...

chapter 14
'HOPE IN WHAT YOU CAN ACHIEVE'

和心会

Randolph Turpin (centre), Annette's father, at Sugar Ray Robinson's reitrement party in New York 1965. Sugar Ray, who is on the far left next to his friend Mohammed Ali, wanted the four fighter he respected the most in the ring with him one last time.

No one understands more than Annette Turpin – daughter of the former world middleweight boxing champion Randolph Turpin – about how karate training can expand the horizons of children and young people. Throughout her career in the National Health Service, Annette has worked as a nurse specialising in child psychiatry, helping guide young people and their families through periods of intense illness and life difficulty. At the same time, she has practised karate for nearly thirty years and now holds a 5th Dan black belt.

Annette advises the Washinkai organisation on child protection issues. I have been privileged to have been her teacher on occasion and have watched her career right from the beginning.

Now a karate instructor herself, she remembers vividly the first time she walked into a dojo in South London in 1986. "I just went to watch and then joined in. I was just blown away by the first lesson. Then for my first national club championships, I remember walking in very much an outsider and being amazed at the presence, performance and discipline of those taking part. It was inspirational. When I took the grading for my first degree black belt in 1993, I realised that it meant more to me than anything else I had achieved until then. There's something about the total effort involved: physical, mental and emotional. It's so testing."

With the combination of her professional background and karate training, Annette still feels inspired to watch how troubled, shy or self-conscious young people can blossom in the dojo. "I don't believe any child is a lost cause. There has to be a hope in what you can achieve. It's about accepting the individual for who they are. Not only that, it's also having someone believe you can amount to something. I remember an instructor telling me: 'You're not as good as you're going to be.' If I thought I could inspire people and excite people like that, then wouldn't it just be fantastic?

"In the karate dojo, you see all abilities and all ages as well as parents training with their own children. I remember

one mum eventually being selected to train with the England squad. Of course, in the dojo, girls do the same as boys. They're just as capable. Everyone has potential.

"It's great to see the incredible transformation of children who are afraid to open their mouths when they first come into the dojo. Too many kids feel useless. They haven't seen themselves as sporty. Then comes the first grading, that orange belt, and they have proof they can achieve something. If you feel you have some skills, then you won't appear vulnerable or weak. You walk in a certain way and how you walk into a room matters: it shows you have confidence, awareness and presence."

Sometimes, not always, karate training can and does

help children who find it difficult to find their way in the school system, family or community – young people, for example, who have problems with co-ordination, concentration or control. They may be given a wide range of clinical labels, but basically they're the wild ones or the difficult ones. Annette puts it this way: "Karate is like brain gym. It does something to children's brains, helps with co-ordination, balance, self-control and ultimately self-respect. I vividly remember the example of one girl suffering from dyspraxia who passed her purple belt grading exam. The look of achievement on her face was unforgettable."

Karate training will never be and should never be a substitute for good parenting, but it can certainly go a long way to giving troubled young people new hope in the possibilities of their lives ... a belief they can amount to something, become more than they ever thought possible.

chapter 15
LIFE SKILLS FOR SOLDIERS, NHS STAFF AND SIXTH FORMERS

和心会

Keep it simple – advice you see and read regularly from professionals in all walks of life. It's especially true in the martial arts. It's also the cornerstone of the life skills classes I run for professionals and school students, especially those who regularly have to confront violence as part of their jobs.

In 2001, I received a call from Major Rob Howells MBE, who had set up the Army Martial Arts Association (AMMA). He asked if I would officiate at the combined martial arts competitions. So I went to help out along with my referee colleagues Paul Hacker and Mike Beasley. Then another call came from Al Curtin of the Royal Navy-Royal Marine Martial Arts Association. That, in turn, led to competition events bringing together all the Armed Services. Today,

Washinkai instructors and referees take part every year in competitions for professional soldiers who practise martial arts for fun and fitness and to keep up their professional skills.

Along the way, I had many informal conversations with troops from the Special Forces and now I have a regular invitation to run informal classes for them in basic karate. I got to know them well. For many years I have had regular meetings with an ex-sergeant in the SAS and have exchanged ideas on how best to take care of yourself in difficult situations.

Unlike the Hollywood image of these elite troops, the British Special Forces I know often look very ordinary. Many of them are small in stature. They blend in. That is one of the qualities that make them so effective. As professionals, they like the pragmatic approach of karate and the martial arts, the idea of maximum effect from minimum effort. That is a guiding principle at the heart of all my teaching. Most times in life, even in conflict zones, the situation does not warrant the "all guns blazing" approach so much loved by film directors. Sometimes you need the soft way, a way of defusing potentially violent situations with simple techniques that make it absolutely clear you will not be cowed or bullied by an aggressor.

Some of Britain's service men in action at the Inter-Services Karate Championships.

You don't need to stomp around and break bones to protect

and defend yourself and your loved ones. That is important to remember if you come across violence regularly at work, as is the case with doctors and nurses in the National Health Service.

During the year 2011-2012 in England alone, there were nearly 60,000 attacks on doctors, nurses and reception staff working in hospitals, clinics and even in everyday GP surgeries. The organisation NHS Protect says there's been a steep rise in assaults by patients whose condition contributes to their violent outbursts. Perhaps patients with learning difficulties or mental health problems, or even just people in pain, find it more difficult to cope with waiting times and delays in treatment. Every hospital casualty department also has to deal with violence from patients who are simply drunk. The National Health Service has always had a problem with out-of-control patients angry at slow treatment in both A&E and GP clinics. Despite increased Government investment in security guards and cameras in hospitals, the problem seems to get worse every year.

Just over twenty years ago, my own GP– who had also been a doctor in the Royal Navy – started practising karate and after a few lessons he said: "This would be good training for the NHS." So I decided to run self-defence awareness courses for GPs, hospital doctors, reception staff and nurses, including the specialist nursing staff who now carry out so many of those essential medical checks we receive when we visit the GP surgery.

The most common form of assault on NHS staff is strangulation. When a violent patient starts to argue with reception staff, the receptionist will often lean over the desk or counter to try to pacify the angry patient. In doing so, the staff unwittingly expose their necks and often lean off balance, making themselves vulnerable to attack. The best defence is the simplest. Don't try anything complicated or fancy. Just grab both the attacker's pinkies, the weakest fingers on our hands, and bend them back quickly and fiercely. Break the fingers if you have to. The attacker will let go immediately.

The important thing is to show aggressive patients, politely but firmly, that you will not be submissive. You must hold yourself and speak with authority. Obviously, a quick self-defence course doesn't turn you into Bruce Lee. But even basic training and awareness helps you not to panic when someone is in your space and in your face. In confrontation, people just freeze. It's natural. They become petrified. That not only causes the victim more damage and injury, but it renders them completely submissive.

If you practise martial arts or self-defence, then you become able to act instinctively to counter attack and move away – to do something quickly to get yourself out of trouble. Medical staff are especially well equipped to know those areas of the body that are most vulnerable to the short, sharp shock of defence: the eyes, the ears, the skin inside the thigh. And of course, the last thing a violent man expects is that a woman – and so many of our frontline health workers are women – will grab his testicles and twist them hard.

Doctors on night calls can find themselves at risk, even if they are accompanied by a driver, and these self-defence awareness courses can make them more street savvy. A heavy duty torch can be an excellent defensive weapon, as can a rolled up newspaper or magazine. Again, keep it simple. Use whatever you have to hand to defend yourself: a bunch of keys can be a very good weapon to help you out of a tight spot.

Dr Brian Ellis understands these issues more acutely than most people. He spent his professional life as a GP in the National Health Service and also holds a fourth-dan black belt in karate within the Washinkai organisation. He says: "Aggression is an everyday occurrence in the NHS. When you use karate as the basis for self-defence awareness classes for medical teams, you're not so much teaching staff to react in a physical way, but teaching them to defuse difficult situations in a supportive atmosphere. Karate gives them the confidence that they don't have to crumple in the face of potential physical aggression. That confidence is

detected by the potential assailant."

With the Sixth Formers who attend my life skills classes, many of the teenagers have just passed their driving test. If you find yourself at night being followed or tail-gated in your car, people often say: "Drive to the nearest police station." But when did you last see a police station open after six in the evening? Instead, head straight for the nearest twenty-four hour petrol station, which will have cameras, bright lights and attendants. Make a mental note of where they are. The bullies will disappear very quickly. The teenagers I teach are sometimes confronted on the street by thugs demanding their mobile phones. It happens all the time, but the students themselves tend not to want to talk about it. If you're a natural victim, you give off the

signs: shoulders hunched and head down. However scared you may feel inside, be assertive and positive. Shock the thieves. Say: "No – fuck off!" That's a shock in itself.

If you're approached by an aggressor in the street, make a noise. Scream your head off. Don't shout – no one takes any notice. But if you scream "Fire!", then that's when the curtains open. Don't be a willing victim; don't look like a natural victim waiting to be attacked. Be assertive. You can't necessarily rely on your best friend. They may be thinking: "Thank God it's not me." Again, that's just human nature. You can't rely on anyone else.

In the affluent areas of south-east England, where I do a great deal of my martial arts teaching, teenagers think they won't be at the receiving end of abuse on the streets. Many don't think they'll ever be in danger. Some of the teenagers from wealthy families think their parents will get them out of every sort of trouble. For 99 per cent of the high school students I teach, these life skills classes are an eye opener. But the head teachers are very supportive. They know most of the students are in for a shock when they reach the big wide world.

The memory of being bullied as a schoolboy is still very much alive for friend and colleague Neville Smith, now a Seventh Dan black belt with Washinkai karate and an expert in self-defence. Every year at our summer training camps, he and fellow karate instructor Neil Benton, Sixth Dan, run highly popular classes in how teenagers and students can take care of each other on the street. "I was bullied as a kid," Neville says. "I had just turned eleven and a bunch of gang members used to give me a regular kicking. Who knows why? Maybe I wasn't in the in-crowd. Perhaps my nose was too big or my clothes un-cool. I was in the Scouts. Could it have been that?

"Anyway, one day I ran into a working men's club to get away from the gang and found a karate class. At first it didn't make any difference. I tried to fight back and still got beaten up. When I asked my karate instructor why it wasn't working, he said: 'You need to train harder and more often.' So I did. And I'll never forget the look on the face of one of

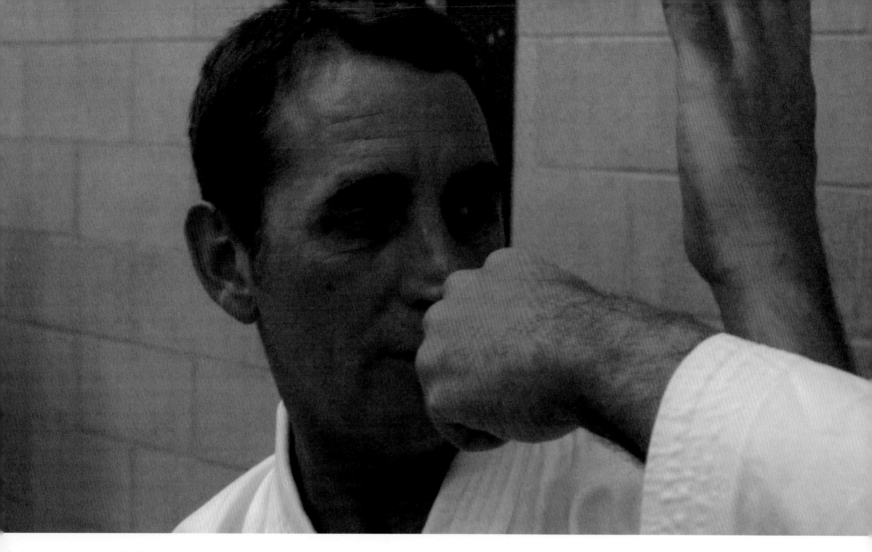

Cool under pressure: Sensei Neville Smith (7th Dan)

those gang members when I stood up to him and punched him."

Over the years, I have tracked down almost every member of the gang that tormented me as a schoolboy. With each of them, I hit them just once. Then they know – what they did wasn't all right."

chapter 16
WHAT FUTURE FOR KARATE IN ENGLAND?

和心会

Chris Thompson and Yoshinobu Ohta, Japan 2008

The fighting arts take their place without question in every Olympic Games, including boxing, judo and tae-kwon-do. But not karate! At first glance that might seem strange, given that karate is now firmly established as a martial art and competitive sport in almost every country in the world and has hundreds of thousands of followers and practitioners. In reality, the karate world is everywhere divided by factional struggles and petty jealousies among different styles and personalities. Leadership seems fragmented and weak. Throughout the half century that karate has been practised in England, its popularity has inevitably gone through peaks and troughs. Now I believe it is in urgent need of reform.

Just over eighteen years ago, I began a close friendship with the head of Shotokan karate in Britain, Sensei Yoshinobu Ohta. He is chief instructor and chairman of the Japan Karate Association in England and in great demand across the UK and Europe as a teacher and interpreter of Shotokan, the most widely practised karate style in the world. Before taking up his present role, he worked as a personal assistant to the legendary Keinosuke Enoeda, the so-called Tiger of Shotokan, and then succeeded Enoeda when he died in 2003. As a university student, Sensei Ohta trained with some of the great modern masters of Japanese karate and then graduated from the highly prestigious JKA instructors' course in Tokyo. He has worked at the top of Shotokan karate in England for more than thirty years and has now lived in England longer than his native Japan.

All this makes Ohta perfectly placed by background and experience to take an expert and dispassionate view of the state of English karate. He believes – as I do – that we need to create a better, stronger future for karate in this country. Karate-ka in the UK can and should be among the best in the world again. High on Ohta's priority list for reform is a series of strategic changes that have the power to revolutionise karate in England:

- Creating a national coaching qualification accepted by all styles of karate and recognised by the Government and Sport England.
- Promoting greater co-operation between different styles, potentially training together and sharing techniques and kata that have a common history.
- Reversing the declining popularity of karate by attracting more teenagers and university students and doing more to ensure that a higher proportion of students stay with karate after taking their black belt.
- Building a national cadet squad that will become the basis of a world-beating England karate team of the future.

At the heart of his proposals is the re-establishment of trust in the leadership of karate and the creation of a governing body that will speak with one voice and win respect at the highest levels of British life, government and society. Of course, he understands from personal experience that the changes we both dream of will take time and struggle. English karate has much to learn from his life story and experience.

As soon as he arrived in Britain in 1982, Ohta suffered from the endless rivalries between different governing bodies in British martial arts. At that time, there was also a backlash and prejudice against Japanese instructors. Rising English

228

stars of karate thought they didn't need them. Incredibly for a man who had studied karate with some of the leading sensei in Japan, he was accused of not teaching "proper" Shotokan. "For three to five years, people said I wasn't teaching Shotokan, but I didn't care what people said. Yes, I almost gave it up, but I didn't want to give it up. I tried not to think about it too much. Thinking a lot doesn't always make things better. You just have to keep going. The only way to prove myself was to just keep going my way. You need patience. I could not open people's minds and say, 'This is my way' I just had to wait. If people liked me, they would follow me. There's no other way."

Of course, they did follow him and Ohta's way became increasingly popular. In clubs from the Orkney Islands to the far South West of England and throughout Europe, he was in demand as a visiting instructor, grading examiner and interpreter of Shotokan. Most days, he also taught twice a day at the JKA England headquarters in London. While the leaders of Shotokan in England squabbled among themselves about who represented the "true way", a growing number of ordinary students were attracted by the speed and realism of Ohta's karate.

The Young Tiger of Shotokan, Sensei Yoshinobu Ohta

For a teacher who learnt his fighting arts at the heart of the JKA in Tokyo, he was remarkably open to learning from the best of other styles. "In kumite, you use the best technique.

You can use any technique you like to win. Obviously, in competition Shotokan people sometimes meet Wado Ryu people and so on, so they must know other styles."

Part of this point of view can be explained by the fact that Ohta was such a competitive fighter as a teenager in Japan. At that stage of his life, winning was probably more important than correct form. He also arrived in England at a time when the UK had some of the best fighters in the world, champions like Ticky Donovan, Vic Charles and Geoff Thompson.

The Ohta way is much, much more than the will to win. In his interpretation, "dynamic" and "traditional" are not in opposition to each other. "I tried to make a different

kind of karate. Power and speed sometimes don't work on their own. Rather than just hitting hard and breaking an opponent, we started to think about different kinds of technique, different directions, different footwork and movement. It's not enough to be just strong and fast. You also need timing and body technique."

Even when Ohta became the New Tiger in 2003 following the death of Sensei Enoeda, who had grown to be his mentor and friend, he was surrounded by controversy. Shortly before his appointment, Ohta had passed the examination for sixth dan in front of the JKA's most senior grading committee in Tokyo. Higher dan grades in England felt they should have inherited Enoeda's crown, and so the faction fighting intensified even further. Ohta loves karate, but he hates karate politics. "There's always too much politics."

Now as the head of JKA in England, Sensei Ohta shares with me concerns about the decline in numbers within all martial arts in England. "We are 60 per cent children. Some groups are 90 per cent children and most of those disappear after black belt. We have to think about how to keep the children. Gradings are a problem. You can't just give a grading as a present. Competition may be one way to keep children interested: friendly matches with other styles of karate. Of course, the leadership of karate is very fragile at the moment and that makes it even worse. Children and parents want people they can trust. It's very sad."

At the same time, karate can never be a substitute for good parenting. "With younger children, parents send their children for exercise or respect or discipline. I believe if you have no discipline at home, you cannot teach it in the club. Parents must instil discipline in the beginning. Karate cannot do everything. Good parents make good children. Children learn from a good family how to discipline themselves, how to learn things.

"Older children have their own agenda. They want to learn. In our association, there are not many sixteen to eighteen year olds. It's a very important age to develop mind and body. In Japan, karate is very popular with that age group. But in this country, there are so many exams or boyfriends or girlfriends. People leave.

"Twenty is not too late to start, but not many people join at that age. At university, there are not many students doing karate. There used to be hundreds of them, but no longer. Then after university, they get a job or they're just busy. I find it very, very sad."
If England is to become a real force again in international karate competition, then that success will depend on a new generation of young and committed students. "I'd like to see the English team win the world," says Ohta. "Why not? It's happened before. But no one is competing at cadet level. Why is there no England cadet team entering international competition? If you have no children, you will have no seniors."

Is it too late to put in place the reforms suggested by Sensei Ohta? Perhaps it is, but I believe those reforms are still worth fighting for and urgently needed.

As things stand, no one needs any formal qualification or training to set himself up as a karate instructor. You can buy some insurance, hire a hall, hang a banner outside describing yourself as the chief instructor of "Go-To Karate" and there's nothing in the law or the rules to stop you. If I send my children to swimming lessons, I can be sure that the instructors have been trained and accredited by the Amateur Swimming Association. If your son or daughter wants to play with the local football club, then that club and its staff and volunteers have to be registered by the Football Association. It's time that karate moved into the 21st Century and set up a national coaching academy with an instructor qualification recognised by the Government and respected by the public. After a transition period, any karate club run by unqualified coaches could be shut down and prosecuted.

In Washinkai karate and in other leading styles, all instructors are trained and monitored constantly and submit themselves to regular security checks. We have a rigorous grading syllabus recognised by Japan as a complete martial arts system. We have child protection officers and a host of policies to ensure that all students are taught safely and with respect. But as Sensei Ohta puts it: "There are too many Mickey Mouse instructors out there." For the future good of karate and the students who practice it, the rules and standards must be tightened up urgently.

It's also time to stop the faction fighting between different karate styles and different governing bodies. We need

a single governing body that can speak clearly with one powerful voice to Government, the public and the Olympic movement.

Throughout the 1990s and beyond, there was a relatively short period of harmony. The English Karate Governing Body (EKGB) represented all styles everywhere across the country. I served as chairman of the technical committee of the EKGB and then as technical director for the new unified EKGB Limited. At the time, both these organisations were the only karate governing bodies recognised by the English Sports Council. Prior to the EKGB, karate was splintered into many opposing factions, as it is now.

Four times a year, I travelled to Coventry for EKGB meetings and regularly shared the car journey with Sensei Mick

Dewey, chief instructor of a large Shotokan organisation in southern England, and Sensei Dave Hazard, a leading member of the same group – both of them gifted and successful teachers of karate. Everyone wanted to see English karate unified, strong and well run and worked hard to achieve that. But in the end, dissent broke out again. The grand old men who run English karate (and they are mostly men!) need to put their house in order once and for all.

We also need to do more to raise the profile of karate in education. In schools throughout the country, karate classes are now an important part of extra-curricular life. But karate can and should also be taught and examined as part of the GCSE and A-level course in Physical Education. We need university sports scholarships for talented young martial artists along the American model. But to achieve all that, there must be recognised training for martial arts coaches, a national coaching academy, an agreed syllabus whatever style of karate is practised and a governing body – approved by the Department for Education and Sport England – that sets, monitors and controls standards.

Until that happens, England will never have another karate team in the world championship finals and karate will never become an Olympic sport. If karate in England cannot put its own house in order and organise itself better, it doesn't deserve to win Olympic medals or world championships.

Sensei Ohta demonstrating application (bunkai) during a course with Washinkai Student Alex Thick.

chapter 17
SPORT OR MARTIAL ART?

和心会

The Washinkai Competition Squad after a successful outing - late 1980s.

Competition training is a vital part of most karate clubs, essential as a way of allowing students to test their skills in combat, overcome their inhibitions and confront their fears. But karate is also a martial art – a complete fighting system which can be used as an effective form of self-defence. If karate is to be any use at all as self-defence, then training must also be highly realistic.

There have been several forms of competition rules used in karate over the past few decades, but the two that have remained consistent are Shobu Ippon and, more recently, the scoring system of the World Karate Federation (WKF).

Shobu Ippon is the original form of competition and was used in Japan before being exported to the rest of the world in the 1950s. It is deemed a highly realistic form of competition, even with its strict rules regarding safety.

The scoring is simple. A half point or wazari is awarded by the referee for a technique deemed powerful enough to damage or wound an opponent, but not strong enough to kill. An ippon (one point) is given for a technique believed strong enough to kill. The competition is won when a fighter achieves an ippon score. This can happen within seconds of the bout starting. Two wazari scores will end a match immediately. At the end of a bout, if one competitor has a wazari, then that fighter will be the winner.

This system, with its various rules, is still seen by many karate-ka as the most realistic form of competition. It is thought to reflect the true spirit of budo (realistic fighting of the samurai). Traditionalists believe that the WKF scoring system is far too unrealistic, with its continuous scoring of potentially weaker techniques.

The WKF rules for competition are far more detailed than Shobu Ippon. Scoring is either ippon (one point), nihon (two points) or sanbon (three points). Dynamic varied technique is encouraged, with high kicks to make it attractive to spectators and, above all, extreme control of techniques (waza) to avoid any serious injury. The WKF rules are there to encourage a more sporting element to

karate, but not to the detriment of good technique. Fitness, strength and good waza are still paramount under WKF rules.

The debate between Shobu Ippon and WKF rules has been going on for years. Many competitors compete in both styles of competition. As an example, Shotokan stylists, who generally stick to Shobu Ippon rules, will often compete under WKF rules if they wish to represent their club, association or country. If karate is ever included as an Olympic sport, it will almost certainly be under WKF competition rules.

But karate is much more than high kicks and competition.

My gut feeling is that training in karate as a martial art is essential. A karate-ka must learn the skills of defending and protecting themselves without weapons in highly realistic training drills. In WKF competition, fighters train to make controlled contact. More than that, the word "art" is crucially important in martial art. Karate is not only about scoring points and winning medals, but has at its heart the kind of continual training that develops wisdom with strength through greater judgment and understanding of oneself and others.

The sporting element appeals to children and young people and is essentially egotistical. Over the last twenty-five years, it has helped to make karate popular among new generations of followers. But fighters who practise only for sport will have nothing left once they are no longer able to move with speed. Perhaps the greatest challenge of all is to avoid the very real temptation of abandoning the traditionalist roots of karate in search of medals alone. That is why Washinkai is a traditional style with kata that are in some cases more than two hundred years old.

Perhaps karate training has become too soft. A lot of people don't want karate to be an Olympic sport. Others want nothing but sport. For me, karate without the values of the martial arts is a selfish waste of time and energy.

chapter 18
WHY WE SHOULD STILL PRACTISE MARTIAL ARTS:

和心会

Everybody is equal in the dojo: Karate competition participants at The Honbu dojo in Somerset.

In some ways, karate makes very old fashioned demands on its followers and practitioners. It needs hard work, commitment and dedication over many years. Sometimes progress seems and is painstaking and slow. Passing the grading exams is never a foregone conclusion. Becoming an expert can take a lifetime. New students dream of achieving the cherished black belt, then realise being a black belt is like becoming a beginner all over again with a new world of expertise waiting to be learned and experienced. Facing an opponent in the dojo and on the competition mat can be and often is frightening. So why bother? To quote my Washinkai colleague and friend Neville Smith, karate can simply "bring out the best in you". Here below is my own list of the top ten benefits that come from dedicating your time to this magical martial art. It's not just my top ten. In forty-five years of teaching karate, these are the benefits students tell me they cherish most about karate.

Fitness and Wellbeing

In the early part of the 20th Century, a Japanese military doctor took one look at the Okinawan teenagers who practised karate and realised they seemed much fitter and stronger than young people in mainland Japan. Nothing much has changed. If you go to a dojo two or three times a week for karate training, you will become fitter and stronger. You don't need a lot of equipment – indeed you can practise karate without any equipment at all. You just need a good instructor and a place to practise regularly. It may be demanding, but karate does give its followers a great sense of well-being.

Self-Confidence

Confidence is a huge benefit for most of the young people who take up karate. In every playground and park in the land, and in many homes and school classrooms, children are bullied, put down and picked on because they are said to have the wrong shape, size, colour, gender or attitude. In the karate dojo everyone is welcome and everyone is equal. In the dojo, something magical does happen:

you work hard, get fit, learn to look after yourself, make friends and then suddenly realise you can walk tall and look the world in the eye.

Self-control

I talked earlier about the student who said he sometimes had to drag himself to karate class with the attitude of a dog going to the vet. The same teenager made another fascinating and very honest observation: "Karate has helped me to learn to control my anger and realise that arguments don't have to be settled in aggressive fashion, but instead by understanding the other person's side of the story." If that kind of understanding could echo around the world, we might have fewer wars. It's one of the many paradoxes of martial arts: learning karate makes you less prone to anger and more likely to find the quiet way to solve problems. Self-control is born of self-confidence.

Self-discipline

The important word here is "self". The only kind of discipline that really works in the long run is a mental and physical regime the student believes in and takes on voluntarily. Karate can never be a substitute for good parenting. But sooner or later, usually sooner, every student understands they have to discipline themselves and work hard to achieve their dreams. Self-discipline is a life skill.

Self-defence

Emily Pankhurst set up a squad of Suffragette women who trained in the Eastern arts of self-defence so they could protect their leader from attack and arrest. They understood a simple and practical lesson in life. At some stage, we all need the confidence and capacity to stand up to bullying and street attack. Karate doesn't turn all its followers into Bruce Lee, but it does give them the knowledge and courage to look after themselves in difficult situations. That is another important life skill.

Self-respect

At the heart of all martial arts is the idea that self-respect is essential to a happy and adventurous life. In turn, this individual self-respect breeds respect for others around us. It is a traditional virtue that does not always sit easily with the relentless individualism of Western society. But if you practise karate for any length of time, respect will become part of your way of life. I believe it can help to make you happy.

Friends and a new kind of family

As we have seen earlier in this book, karate is one of the few sporting activities where families can train together and even sometimes compete together. I have heard and read countless stories of families who find themselves closer to each other through karate. And a dojo is like a good family: people help each other, look out for each other, but also give each other space to grow and improve.

Focus

In a media age of round-the-clock news and non-stop social media, it's easy to lose focus on what is really important. There's too much noise and distraction. On the training mat or the competition arena, faced with an opponent who can do you harm if you don't take avoiding action, then focus becomes a way of being. It's like meditation in action, emptying your mind and senses so you can give all your attention and skill to what is going in the moment of here and now. That is arguably a great life skill.

Commitment

For most beginner students training two or three times a week, it takes four or five years of constant hard work and study to achieve a black belt in karate. Continuing after the first black belt can take a lifetime's devotion. That level of commitment and resilience breed in you the staying power to achieve almost anything in life, whatever the obstacles.

Emotional strength

No one talks about fear very much, but it is there almost every time you face an opponent on the competition mat. It takes inner strength to understand the emotion of fear, how it affects you, how to deal with it and how to take some useful action in spite of it. Learning that gift of strong heartedness in the face of trouble might just be the most important life skill of all.

Flying High: James Gawler and Dan Smith perform the kata Unsu at The Honbu.

chapter 19
WHAT TO LOOK FOR IN A GOOD KARATE CLUB

師範クリス・トンプソン

和心会

Dojo – it means literally "place of the way". It can be anywhere: village hall, school gym, sports centre, a field outdoors in the sun and rain. Washinkai karate in the south west of England has a full-time martial arts dojo created and transformed out of the ruins of abandoned motor garage. The point is not the place itself, but the energy and commitment a student brings to it. Any area or space in which a karate-ka trains becomes, in spirit, a dojo.

A student of karate must at all times show correct etiquette towards the dojo and towards fellow students, sempai (seniors) and sensei. There should be no 'orders' given – merely mutual respect and co-operation between sensei and deshi (pupil).

Discipline is more strict in a properly run dojo than in almost any other situation in modern life, yet the air is not repressive because this discipline is self-imposed.

There are times when students may talk freely and joke and laugh inside the dojo without breaking etiquette.

The new karate student need only behave politely to be in accord with the correct spirit of the dojo.

In practice, this means behaving with respect at all times. Bow when entering or leaving the dojo, wear a clean smart 'gi' or karate suit – take pride in your appearance, acknowledge a senior's help with a bow, behave with good manners towards everyone and be punctual. The point

The Honbu Dojo, Summer 2014. An extensive refurbishment was carried out to improve the facilities currently on offer.

here is not blind obedience to imposed rules, but the understanding that dojo etiquette comes from within as an expression of your own core values. At its best, the dojo can be a source of self-reflection, self-understanding and personal transformation. The discipline and the etiquette, and the wisdom that lies beneath them, somehow help with the journey.

If you are a beginner or the parent of a child who wants to take up karate, how do you choose a good dojo? Most of the time, the choice will be based simply on finding a karate club near your home and family friends. But it's important to make sure the club is right for you or your family.

Ask the instructor if you can sit and watch a class. If the instructor says 'no', just walk away. Even if you don't understand completely what is happening, trust your gut feeling. Is the class professionally run? As mentioned above, all students should show good discipline but in a good club the atmosphere will not be repressive or harsh. Would you or your child feel safe in this dojo? Is the instructor well qualified and trained? Do they have first aid qualifications? Have they had a criminal records check? Do they have insurance? Are they part of a wider organisation which is part of a recognised governing body such as Karate England, the Japan Karate Association or the World Karate Federation? Do the club and its parent organisation have a child protection policy? How does the instructor talk to the children – is he or she respectful towards them? Ask other parents or students about the club. Listen to the tone of the gossip and conversation as karate-ka enter and leave the dojo.

Do the students seem happy? You should be able to tell quite quickly whether a club or organisation is right for you or your family.

The logo of Washinkai karate and the British Traditional Karate Association has seven petals spiralling out from the centre. They reflect the seven elements of perfect technique, but also the seven characteristics of good

Sensei Thompson demonstrating one of the Ohyo Gumites (Semi-Free Fighting) that are peculiar to the Washinkai Style.

karate-ka and good karate clubs. Those qualities are: humility, honesty, responsibility, respect, courtesy, integrity and equanimity. If you feel that a karate club and the members of it display those qualities, then you should be safe to begin your own life adventure in karate.

chapter 20
IS KARATE WORTH THE PAIN?

和心会

Students practising Tenshin-Sho, a kata developed by Sensei Thompson for the Washinkai Style.

My life in karate has been a constant journey of discovery, a real adventure. And my life story in the martial arts has been, quite rightly, as much about the friends and students I have met along the way and what karate has meant for them.

In the end, is karate worth the pain, dedication and commitment of a lifetime's training – and does it have a future? Perhaps the last word should rest with the medical experts.

First Dr Brian Ellis (4th Dan), the GP we met earlier talking about self-defence training for doctors, nurses and medical reception staff.

"I'm sure karate has made me more resilient in coping with life in general. Having confidence in your own ability adds a bit of steel to your character. I started karate in 1996 in my late forties. It was my son who went to karate class first and Chris Thompson said, 'Why don't you do it, too?' I thought, 'You must be joking!'

"But for me, I discovered it ticked a number of boxes. I felt much fitter. It was a friendly, supportive atmosphere. And technically, I felt I could be improving all the time. Like so many things in life, you can always improve yourself.

"There are many mental benefits from physical training in karate. You gain an increased ability to prioritise, to put things in a much better perspective. Through karate, I discovered the zen idea of 'mushin', or better mind, at least a state of 'no mind' where you can empty yourself of all distractions and assumptions and be completely present in the moment, prepared for whatever comes along. Karate keeps the neurological pathways moving, keeps your life energy strong."

Professor Geir Støre (6th Dan) is one of the leading surgeons in Norway and heads the Washinkai karate organisation in Scandinavia. He numbers among his students many gold medallists and national champions.

He believes karate is more needed than ever before.
"As the father of five children and five grandchildren, I

witness with some concern the many hours spent every day staring on both small and big screens. The Norwegian Army (we have compulsory military service) announced recently that their traditional test march had to be reduced from 3,000 metres to 2,000 metres due to a general decline in fitness of young soldiers! As a tournament doctor, I have also observed a drop in quality and standard of present-day contestants compared to earlier decades.

"In the jungle of quick-fix sports offer like spinning, cross training and all the other fads and fashions, is there still a future for traditional karate? If I am optimistic, it is due to the character and wisdom of sensei like Chris Thompson and their breed of good students. Washinkai was established as an open minded organisation in opposition to the obsolete and rigid Japanese-dominated karate structure. I am convinced it is possible to adjust to the demands of future generations without abandoning traditional karate values. I believe the legacy of Washinkai karate will live on."

That legacy already lives on now in the lives and achievements of the many thousands of karate students who chose to travel this road with me over the last forty-five years. For me, it was simply the life I loved ... just magic.

Professor Geir Støre

chapter 21
STILL CRAZY AFTER ALL THESE YEARS

和心会

Over the past forty-five years, karate has given me the life I love. I'm sixty now. I still teach and train. I'm in a dojo running courses somewhere across Britain or Europe several times a week. The dojo feels more like home than almost anywhere else in the world.

And that is the final point really.

I'm delighted you have read this book and followed its story. But karate is for doing, not for talking about. That is a good thing. We live our modern lives too much in our head. Sitting is the new smoking, they say, and we spend a lot of time sitting down watching screens of some sort.

Why not grab some of the action for yourself? Find a good karate club and discover its delights and challenges. The experience will stay with you for the rest of your life.

Why not grab some of the action for yourself and discover the delights and challenges of karate?

BRITISH TRADITIONAL KARATE ASSOCIATION

DOJOKUN

和心会 道場訓

強い精神
美しい心
健康な体

TSUYOI SEISHIN
UTSUKUSHII KOKORO
KENKO NA KARADA

learn with your soul as well as your body